LEADERSHIP IN

HEALTHCARE

Essential Values and Skills

Second Edition

D1405131

LEADERSHIP IN

HEALTHCARE

Essential Values and Skills

Second Edition

Carson F. Dye

ACHE Management Series

Acquisitions editor: Janet Davis; Project manager: Jane Calayag; Cover designer and layout: Scott Miller

Found an error or a typo? We want to know! Please e-mail it to hap1@ache.org, and put "Book Error" in the subject line.

For photocopying and copyright information, please contact Copyright Clearance Center at www.copyright.com or at (978) 750–8400.

Health Administration Press
A division of the Foundation of the American
    College of Healthcare Executives
One North Franklin Street, Suite 1700
Chicago, IL 60606–3529
(312) 424–2800

Contents

Foreword

Michael H. Covert, FACHE
President and Chief Executive Officer
Palomar Pomerado Health

I HAVE HAD the privilege of working and collaborating with Carson Dye for more than 25 years. During this period, we have had the opportunity to observe leaders at different stages of their development in a variety of healthcare settings. The common thread among successful executives has been the core set of values they live by day in and day out. These leaders have an innate ability to translate their beliefs in meaningful and demonstrable ways in the workplace and in their personal lives. They are secure with themselves, their abilities, and their priorities. They know what they stand for, no matter the chaos in the world around them.

These leaders' values work in concert with the culture of their organization, and these values stand strong even amid cultural transformations. It could be said that they have the same knowledge, skill sets, and experiences expected and required by the field, which has always been beset with changes—whether financial, legislative or regulatory, labor related, or political. However, because of their values, these leaders set themselves apart, drawing to them people who relate to these values and who sense that being around these leaders will improve their own abilities. The teams that values-based leaders develop create structures out of ambiguity, manage stress during difficult periods, recognize the strength of group work, and foster environments in which an individual member's contributions are noted and valued.

My experience building my own teams and helping others in this formation process has taught me that values-based leaders make the environment safe for learning and growing. They are compelled to help others become confident leaders, and they understand that the stronger the members of the team, the more effective the team can undertake any challenge.

This book, *Leadership in Healthcare: Essential Values and Skills*, 2nd edition, is a must read (or a first step) for those who want to evaluate their values and enhance their leadership performance. Such a time investment is worthwhile because of the many insights on personal and team values that readers will glean and the many strategies for translating these concepts into practical use. The vignettes, sidebars, self-evaluation questions, and case studies and exercises enable the reader to "connect the dots" internally. In addition, the leadership team section (Part III) allows the reader to step back to analyze his or her team dynamic, including whether the team is satisfactory to its members and whether members contribute to the team's productivity. In essence, the material in this book serves as a strong road map for a leader's current performance and future succession planning.

Ten years after the publication of the first edition, Carson Dye's message about leadership remains fresh and important. Effective stewardship is all about how we leaders interconnect with others to advance our work of making health and healthcare better.

Foreword

Stephen J. O'Connor, PhD, FACHE
Professor, Department of Health Services Administration
School of Health Professions
University of Alabama at Birmingham

LEADERSHIP, LIKE HEALTHCARE, is rooted in values. The American healthcare system is based on the same Judeo-Christian value system that the early colonists brought to the New World from Europe. In fact the painting *Christ Healing the Sick in the Temple*, located in the lobby of the Pennsylvania Hospital (the nation's first hospital), is an iconic cultural artifact portraying these core healthcare values: patient-centered caring, curing, healing, compassion, empathy, and alleviation of suffering. These values are expressed in various new ways through our contemporary, pluralistic healthcare system and have expanded to include preventive and population health. Likewise, leadership at its heart is about personal, team, and organizational values.

Leadership in Healthcare: Essential Values and Skills, 2nd edition, demonstrates how successful leadership is anchored in well-understood values and encourages the reader to maximize leadership capabilities by developing and practicing a suitable personal value system. Carson Dye combines leadership theory, empirical research, the experience of healthcare executives, and the sage wisdom of leadership experts into a comprehensive and highly readable book. The text is replete with relevant and important literature citations, vignettes and cases from leadership practice, consciousness-raising discussion questions, self-assessment instruments, and quotations that reinforce and instill a deep understanding of the overall leadership concept. The book explains essential principles, theories, and perspectives without being ponderous or impenetrable. Moreover, it provides the reader with a broad conceptualization of what excellent leadership can be and how to go about achieving it.

Leadership in Healthcare: Essential Values and Skills is an excellent text for graduate and undergraduate health administration programs or as supplemental reading for courses in organization theory and behavior. It is also of value to students in executive education programs and to practicing healthcare managers and executives who are seeking to sharpen their leadership skills. Leadership, however, is not limited to those occupying management and executive positions. Clinicians also recognize that true leadership skills are needed today more than ever. As such, many clinical education programs have started to add instruction in leadership to increase their value and to differentiate themselves from competitors. This book is also appropriate for leadership seminars and courses geared for clinicians.

Carson Dye is to be applauded for writing and updating this eminently useful book on what is inarguably the most critical competency needed by healthcare leaders today.

Preface

TEN YEARS HAVE passed since I wrote *Leadership in Healthcare: Values at the Top*. Much has changed in the world, in American society, and in the U.S. healthcare system and its leadership. Yet much remains the same, including the following realities:

1. *Effective leadership is difficult to define.* So many "definitive" leadership books exist, but so few articulate the principles underlying effective leadership.
2. *The ethics of leaders is on the decline.* Power can corrupt, which is evident from the much-reported unethical and criminal activities of top executives in many industries. When inappropriate conduct is committed in healthcare, it not only erodes the public's trust but also threatens patients' safety and lives.
3. *The constant stresses in healthcare cause burnout and change of careers.* As a search consultant, I am acutely aware of leaders' frustrations and uneasiness about the rapid pace of change in the industry. Many of them leave the field as a result, while others struggle through these problems, tired, dejected, and pessimistic.
4. *Leadership development is not a top priority.* Although many senior executives express an interest in professional growth and development, they devote little time and funds to this pursuit.

This paradox is apparent when leadership development becomes the first to get cut from the organizational budget. The current economic downturn becomes another excuse (next to limited time) for overlooking development opportunities.

5. *Effective leaders are almost always values driven.* Those who rely only on hard data and measurable standards often say that values are vague contributors to effectiveness because they cannot be quantified. However, a review of empirical research, coupled with my observations and constant contact with executives, reveals that values are cited by highly effective leaders as major factors of their success.

6. *Effective leadership can be learned.* Some people are "born" leaders. They possess and live by deep, unwavering values. They have a natural ability to interact with and lead others. However, these qualities can be learned by people who are not born with such talents. Becoming aware of the need for learning and practicing a sensitive, practical, and appropriate value system is the first step toward becoming a world-class leader.

We now live in a more frenzied, Internet-driven culture, where technology gives to but also takes away from our daily lives. While smartphones—Blackberrys, iPhones, and the like—have allowed us instant access to other people and to enormous amounts of information, they have shrunk our chances for face-to-face communications. And while social media—Twitter, Facebook, LinkedIn, and the like—have enabled us to network, stay in touch, and even make "friends" from distant locations (something unimaginable in 1999), they have also introduced unique (also unimaginable in 1999) challenges in the workplace. Although the Internet age in healthcare has made some veteran executives say that interactions are "not as fun as they used to be," it does attract and excite the younger leaders among us.

We now live in a post-9/11 world and are amid two wars. The political, social, and economic uncertainties we face manifest in our healthcare facilities, exacerbating the crises organizational leaders must solve every day. Emergency departments continue to be the primary providers for the uninsured and underinsured; a shortage in workers, allied health professionals, physicians, and even clinical educators is threatening the availability and quality of care; advances in medical technology and pharmaceuticals are ramping up the cost of care; and the American public's scrutiny of the industry has gotten louder and clearer. Although not entirely new or insurmountable, these challenges add even more pressure to the already strained healthcare workforce and its leaders.

Although much progress has been attained in the industry, much still needs to be accomplished. This is the environment in which the second edition of *Leadership in Healthcare* is truly effective.

THE INTENT OF THIS BOOK

My goals for this edition are the same as the goals for the first edition:

1. Raise leaders' awareness about values and their meaning.
2. Posit that values play a major role in leaders' effective performance.
3. Recommend practical strategies for living by those values at work and at home.

Judging by the strong reception to and enduring support for the first edition, this book has filled a latent hunger for discussion about values-based leadership, something that even I did not anticipate. The need for such a discussion is not confined to the healthcare executive world; it is also demanded by graduate and undergraduate programs as well as other professional-education providers. The following that this book has garnered has prompted me to present an updated edition that reflects our drastically changed environment.

Changes to the New Edition

This edition remains true to its original premise. However, to better illustrate and highlight the concepts, we have added new elements and expanded the discussions. These additions facilitate teaching, dialogue, and self-reflection. The book now includes the following:

- Opening vignettes that reflect workplace situations
- New and revised strategies and examples
- Sidebars that support the discussions
- New or expanded treatment of the concepts of servant leadership, change makers, employee engagement, emotional intelligence, and groupthink
- Cases and exercises that stimulate reader response
- Suggested readings and updated references
- Online teaching materials for instructors and professors

Content Overview

The book has two forewords—one by Michael H. Covert, FACHE, president and CEO of Palomar Pomerado Health in San Diego, and another by Stephen J. O'Connor, PhD, FACHE, professor at the University of Alabama at Birmingham. The rationale here is to represent the perspectives of the book's main audience, which is composed of healthcare executives and health administration educators and students.

The book is divided into four parts. Part I—Leadership in Healthcare—contains chapters 1 through 3 and sets the current stage on which the industry and its leaders perform their roles. Part II—Personal Values—includes chapters 4 through 10 and catalogs the key values that influence the leader's behaviors, priorities, thought processes, and actions. Part III—Team Values—comprises chapters 11 through 14 and explores the values that guide a leadership team. Part IV—Evaluation—encompasses chapters 15 through 17 and provides tools for assessing team values and effectiveness and careers at all stages. Chapter 18 is written by Jared Lock, PhD, licensed industrial and organizational psychologist and president of Carr & Associates. This contribution is a research-based response to and support of the hypotheses submitted in the book.

Three appendixes are included. Appendixes A through C are tools for evaluating the leader, the team, and the self. The self-evaluation questions in each chapter are designed to challenge current practices and long-held notions about leadership, while all examples (both real and fictional) serve to encourage appropriate behavior as well as to acknowledge that such model behavior is a multistep, multiyear process that requires willingness, hard work, and other people.

Quotations from various leadership and organizational experts are peppered within the text, giving credence to the concepts discussed.

Online Instructor Materials

The following materials are available to instructors and professors who adopt this book for classroom use:

1. PowerPoints for each chapter
2. List of discussion questions
3. List of leadership websites

To access these resources, please e-mail hap1@ache.org.

CONCLUSION

I have worked in the field for almost 40 years now, but I continue to learn about and be fascinated by healthcare leadership. I still ask the questions I began posing years ago: What is leadership? What makes some leaders more effective than others? How can I improve my own leadership skills?

Although this book is not a complete treatise on leadership, it does explore concepts that will cause you to reflect on your own and others' value system, behaviors, mind-set, actions, goals, and performance. I hope it communicates three messages:

1. Effective leadership is needed now more than ever.
2. Values-based leadership can be learned.
3. Values are a primary contributor to great leadership performance.

The rest, as Lao Tzu said, is up to you.

Carson F. Dye, FACHE
December 2009

Acknowledgments

MY ALMOST 40-YEAR healthcare career has been an amazing journey. Much like Dorothy in *The Wizard of Oz*, I have traveled with my own group of scarecrows, tin men (and women), and lions. Each of these extraordinary people, as well as every step and destination we took, has taught me lessons, and I am appreciative of all of them.

To me, much of leadership is about learning and growth. Several CEOs gave me significant opportunities for just that, including Sister Mary George, Michael Covert, Don Cramp, and the late Dr. Lonnie Wright. Other CEOs and senior executives have had ample influence on my thinking, including Steven Mickus, Scott Malaney, and Bill Linesch. Working alongside Kam Sigafoos, Bill Sanger, Dr. Greg Taylor, Gene Miyamoto, the late Dr. Ed Pike, Mike Gilligan, Mark Hannahan, Mark Elliott, Walter Mclarty, Gretchen Patton, and Randy Schimmoeller provided me with a demonstration of superior leadership.

My work as an executive search consultant puts me into daily contact with outstanding leaders. These clients and candidates practice values-based leadership, and many ideas in this book come directly from them. My own experience as an executive has given me ample opportunity to study leadership practices, just as my experience in teaching does. Conducting workshops and webinars for healthcare associations and other organizations as well as having served as an adjunct faculty member for various universities have further honed my understanding of leadership concepts.

I have said it before, and I will say it again: Our field is blessed with the contributions of Health Administration Press (HAP), which produces relevant and high-quality publications. Specifically, I thank Janet Davis, acquisitions manager at HAP, for her support of the second edition. Janet helped me reach out to reviewers of the book. I also want to recognize and thank Jane Calayag, who edited this version and made it so much better. Jane has very ably worked with HAP for a long time and represents the excellence that we enjoy as ACHE affiliates.

Special thanks must go to my friend and colleague Andy Garman, with whom I have coauthored two books. Andy helped me with the academic side of this edition, reviewing the manuscript and providing reference material. Jared Lock, another friend and colleague, wrote Chapter 18 of the book as he did in the last edition. Stephen Mansfield provided great insight into the lessons of hope and its impact on leadership. I also had several very special friends who toiled with me on the content and the revision of a book that has, over the past ten years, continued to show great life and purpose. I must thank and acknowledge Andy Garman, Jared Lock, Steve O'Connor, Scott Malaney, and Steve Mickus.

To work and serve in such a distinctive field as healthcare is a calling and a blessing. Healthcare has so many devoted servant leaders who deserve much credit and acknowledgment. I want to pay special recognition to the many men and women in uniform, particularly those who serve in the Army, Air Force, Navy Medical Service Corps, and Medical and Nursing Corps. David Rubenstein, Paul Williamson, Kathy Van Der Linden, Steve Wooldridge, Kyle Campbell, and many more of our military healthcare leaders epitomize servant leadership, commitment, and personal sacrifice. I am fortunate to have worked with many of them over the years. I salute and thank them.

Now it's time to articulate my most important acknowledgment: I am grateful for my family. My family, whom I absolutely love and respect, keeps me sincere and humble ("We don't pay to hear you speak, Dad," as one of my daughters has said) and gives me purpose, joy, and strength. I thank them for tolerating my physical absence (when I have to be away from home) as well as my mental absence (when my mind is so preoccupied). I am so appreciative of my four magnificent daughters—Carly, Emily, Liesl, and Blakely—and my great son-in-law, Jeremy. They were willing to read my work, and I thank them for that. Of special note is that Liesl took on the roles of editor-in-chief and graphic designer (she created all the exhibits that accompanied the original manuscript). Liesl, thanks very much. Finally, my wife, Joaquina, deserves special thanks. She continues to be supportive, tolerant, a guiding light, and a stellar soul mate. She has always been there, my comforting constant. I am blessed to have the love of all these special people beside me.

Back to Oz for a moment. In the musical *Wicked*, the story of the witches in the *Wizard of Oz*, these words are shared between Glinda, the good witch, and Elphaba, the "bad" witch:

I've heard it said
That people come into our lives for a reason
Bringing something we must learn
And we are led
To those who help us most to grow
If we let them
And we help them in return
Well, I don't know if I believe that's true
But I know I'm who I am today
Because I knew you.

I can say the same for all the leaders I have known. And I hope the leaders who read this book will hear these words spoken about them.

PART I

LEADERSHIP IN HEALTHCARE

CHAPTER 1

The Leadership Imperative

University Hospital is hosting an annual reception for its retired employees. Jonathan Sneed, the hospital's chief executive officer (CEO) in the 1960s and 1970s, is one of the special guests. Now in his 80s, Jonathan remains sharp as he sits at a table with Elizabeth Jankowski, the current CEO. The two are discussing the evolution of healthcare management.

Jonathan: Elizabeth, your challenges are more complex than those we tackled more than 40 years ago. Back then, we thought our issues were insurmountable! But I suspect that 25 years from now, you will think your problems now are simple. There is one constant necessity for a leader throughout the years, however. That is, leaders have to be constantly learning and adjusting their skills and knowledge. They always have to anticipate what is coming just past the horizon. This leadership quality has kept this hospital at the forefront and contributed to its great reputation as a learning organization.

Elizabeth: Great point! I do get concerned sometimes about some of our leaders. In fact, last week at our senior council meeting, we talked about how so many of us have become so busy that we have not been able to invest the time in leadership education.

Jonathan: Watch out for that. Not keeping up with the trends and the new realities is like not changing the oil in your car regularly. You won't see the negative effects until it is too late.

"IT WAS THE best of times, it was the worst of times," wrote Charles Dickens in his classic book, *A Tale of Two Cities*. The same can be said of constantly evolving healthcare.

Consider some of the realities (both good and bad) in the industry that confront healthcare leaders today:

- Growing number of uninsured
- Uncertain implications of healthcare reform
- Pressures to invest in electronic health record systems and other clinical/information technologies
- Aging of the population and changes in worker and patient ethnic/cultural demographics
- Higher expectations from consumers
- Professional shortages and decreasing recruitment pools
- Public calls for transparency and accountability, and growth of regulations

These challenges, and those yet to come, are exactly why the leadership imperative exists. The leadership imperative is the need for healthcare executives to enhance their understanding of the forces at play in the industry and the way they manage through these changes. Simply, the healthcare industry, its workers, and the people it serves need leaders who can rebuild trust, restore efficient processes, and ensure quality through uncertain environmental trends and practices, societal and economic flux, and organizational transitions.

EVOLVING ENVIRONMENT

Healthcare's evolution has brought not just improvements. In fact, it has created inefficiencies and disorganization. However, it has also ushered in more jobs, better operating standards and clinical outcomes, life-saving advances, focus on patients and disease management, improved services, and new sources of revenue, among other things.

Current trends (listed in Exhibit 1.1) and common obstacles (discussed later in the chapter) shape the healthcare environment within which workers function and services are provided. In this landscape, physician–organization relations continue to be among the most challenging issues, along with strategic conflicts that could result from mergers or other steps to gain economies of scale or increase market share. Such conflicts may derail the flow of decisions and disrupt patient services.

Amid changes and problems, healthcare leaders plow through. Some are weary and doubtful of their ability to rebuild trust and continue to guide their organizations. Some, however, are energized by the challenges. When asked about the current state of the industry, several healthcare executives made the following comments:

Exhibit 1.1 Current Trends in Healthcare

- Growing number of uninsured
- Increased emphasis on patient safety and quality
- Diminished revenue sources and decreased reimbursement
- Uncertain implications of healthcare reform
- Pressures to invest in electronic health record systems and other clinical/information technologies
- Demands to hold down costs
- Closer scrutiny of pay-for-performance schemes
- Aging of the population and changes in worker and patient ethnic/ cultural demographics
- Higher expectations from consumers
- Professional shortages and decreasing recruitment pools
- Need for building renovation/construction and equipment purchase
- Rise of social media, Internet commerce, and wireless functionality
- Advances in pharmaceuticals, genomics, and medical interventions
- Public calls for transparency and accountability, and growth of regulations
- Physician integration and alignment, including the employment of physicians

---

- "These are very tough times to be leading a hospital, but I would not have it any other way. This is a good test of my leadership."

- "Well, when the going gets tough, the tough get going—that is certainly true today. I am really up for the challenge."

- "After 35 years in this field, I thought I had seen it all, but the changes keep coming. I am OK with that but it certainly gets tiring many days."

- "I have a better view and sense of direction here at the top. But I am concerned about my middle managers who are down in the trenches. I need to do whatever I can to help them keep holding on."

As these responses articulate, this is an exciting time to be a leader in healthcare.

COMMON OBSTACLES AND IMPERATIVE ACTIONS

Aside from coping with the current realities of the industry, healthcare leaders also navigate the common obstacles of running a multifaceted operation. In this section, these obstacles are listed along with an appropriate imperative action. An imperative action is a step that a leader may take to overcome the obstacle.

Obstacle 1: Organizations Today Are More Complex

Forty years ago, healthcare organizations were structured simply. Freestanding hospitals, private doctor's offices, nursing homes, and local pharmacies were the most ubiquitous embodiments of organizations. Healthcare *systems* did not exist, nor did integrated delivery networks and nursing home chains, and few mergers and acquisitions took place. Physicians were not employed by health systems; instead, they ran small, independent practices.

A hospital was not a conglomerate; it existed solely to provide care for the hospitalized patient. Therefore, its leaders were not mired in the politics of multiple business partners or the bureaucracy of multiple service lines. A hospital's mission and vision were clear.

> A hospital is only a pile of bricks until people walk in in the morning. Yet it is amazing how this prime reality is forgotten, and how secondarily people are treated.
>
> —V. Clayton Sherman (1993)

"The more complex the system, the less efficient its operation" is an adage that is true of today's healthcare systems. Decreased efficiency results in less satisfaction not only for the system's patients but also for its workers. Complex systems exhaust their leaders and their resources because they require more attention and focus.

Imperative action: Restore the simplicity of the healthcare organization by clarifying its structure, mission and vision, and future direction.

Obstacle 2: Employee Commitment, Engagement, and Loyalty Are Low

Opinion surveys continue to reveal that employee commitment and engagement are decreasing, while unionization efforts are increasing. In his book *The Human Equation,* Jeffrey Pfeffer (1998) states that job security is one of the most important elements of a high-performance work environment. For a long time, the healthcare industry offered just that: job security. Employees, in turn, showed their appreciation for this security by being loyal to the organization. Employees stayed at their jobs longer, performed harder and better, recommended family members and friends to apply for open positions, missed fewer workdays, and participated more in the activities of the organization. Gallup (2009a) has developed a well-known employee engagement tool and has shown that engaged employees are more productive.

Today, even the hardiest healthcare systems cannot ensure jobs for their employees. One CEO suggested that the high levels of trust between management and staff that once existed in the healthcare industry may never return: "I remember the first time I faced a room full of hospital employees who were to be laid off. That was 15 years ago, and I personally talked to all of them. However, the last three times my organization has laid employees off, I did not even go to the sessions. I was told that it was legally risky and that it could be better handled by our human resources staff. We handed the laid-off employees to an outplacement firm. I feel like I abandoned them and feel really bad, but I don't know what to do about it."

Imperative action: Enlist the support of strong employees by boosting trust levels and encouraging their participation in organizational initiatives, such as by giving them decision-making roles.

Obstacle 3: Physicians Are Generationally Fragmented and Are Dissatisfied with the Industry

Physicians age 55 and older have different expectations from those who are just beginning medical practice. Older physicians have witnessed the growth of managed care and the eventual drops in reimbursement. They have experienced financial and legal challenges to their role as the "captain of the ship" in patient care. They mourn the disappearance of the club-like atmosphere of medicine, filled with people with the same concerns and priorities. Many even regret having entered the profession.

Younger physicians, on the other hand, have different expectations. Most, if not all, of them begin their careers with enormous student loan debts (some estimates suggest $150,000 or more), so they desire stable employment with set hours and a set salary. In addition, younger physicians believe that medicine is only one part of their life, while older physicians put most of their life's focus on medicine. This divergent perspective, as well as work style, has caused tension between these two groups (Berthold 2008).

The practice of employing physicians, which was the trend in the 1990s, has returned. While in the 1990s, hospitals and health systems hired doctors in response to capitated care financing, today the reason is a combination of physicians' pursuit of a more secure employment (as opposed to the difficulty and expense of private practice and the high rates of malpractice insurance) and the organizations' need for physician loyalty (Merritt, Hawkins & Associates 2007). Although physician employment can help to align common interests and goals, it may also reduce the physicians' autonomy and complicate their decision making. As a result, physicians, even employed ones, may end up losing faith and loyalty in the organization. If given a choice, many physicians would rather have another physician as the leader of the organization, as this actual sentiment from a hospital physician board member seconds: "We seem to have forgotten our patients in our drive to build a bigger, more comprehensive healthcare system. At least having a physician as our CEO would bring back that patient focus."

> By any objective measure, the amount of significant, often traumatic, change in organizations has grown tremendously over the past two decades. Powerful macroeconomic forces are at work here, and these forces may grow even stronger over the next few decades. As a result, more and more organizations will be pushed to reduce costs, improve the quality of products and services, locate new opportunities for growth, and increase productivity.
>
> —John Kotter (1996)

Dissatisfaction with the industry is driving many physicians into management. Physician membership in both the American College of Physician Executives and the American College of Healthcare Executives is growing. Graduate schools throughout the country have developed management programs targeted at physicians. Many physicians enrolled in these courses are motivated by their dissatisfaction with how healthcare organizations are managed. These doctors seek to improve these facilities' operations and services.

Imperative actions: Improve relations with the physician collective. Handle physician employment skillfully. Consider that more and more physicians are qualified to fill leadership roles.

Obstacle 4: Patients Are Dissatisfied with the Industry

Staggering healthcare costs, high insurance premiums or lack of insurance, poor quality of care, limited access to care, and lack of attention or information from providers are just some concerns that cause patient dissatisfaction. Many patient safety advocates, including the Institute for Healthcare Improvement, have raised the level of awareness about dissatisfaction and have pushed various quality practices. Some progress has been made in this regard, but unfortunately, it is just one of the many areas that need to be addressed.

Many healthcare systems have grown so large that patients report a lack of responsiveness similar to that experienced with large corporations. One educated patient compared her experiences with one health system to "calling an 800 customer-service number in the middle of the night on Sunday." In a consumer-driven healthcare market, this type of treatment could lead to loss of revenue, at best, and loss of patient trust, at worst.

Imperative actions: Address patient concerns, improve quality of care and consumer service, and establish a good relationship with the community you serve.

Obstacle 5: Succession Planning Is Not a Priority for Some Retiring Leaders

An increasing number of baby boomer executives will retire in the next few years. Despite these retirement plans, many leaders have not developed a succession plan to ensure that their transition is handled effectively.

New-generation leaders are ready and waiting for their opportunity to learn and grow in these management roles. Many are aware of the leadership imperative and are confident and excited about the future, although some are fearful of the current trends.

Imperative action: Invest time and resources into succession planning and leadership development programs to ensure that the new generation of leaders will make the significant inroads and positive contributions needed for high-quality patient care and service to our communities.

CONCLUSION

In *The Dilbert Principle*, creator Scott Adams (1996) writes: "The most ineffective workers are systematically moved to the place where they can do the least damage: management." Although this sentiment certainly does not characterize most leaders, it reflects the public's jaded perception. And, although it was written almost 20 years ago, the message still holds true. Heeding the leadership imperative and taking preventive measures, as suggested in this chapter, are the only ways to invalidate and combat these negative perceptions.

✳   ✳   ✳

———————— **Self-Evaluation Questions** ————————

✳   Do I view myself as a leader? If so, is my goal to bring about needed change or, in the words of one CEO, "to build palaces and monuments to my legacy"?

✳   Do I view leadership as an act, a process, or a skill?

✳   Do I, and other leaders I know, think that a leadership imperative exists today?

✳   Have I observed any significant shifts and trends within the industry and popular culture that affect leadership in my organization?

✳   Does it seem more difficult to lead and manage change today?

SUGGESTED READINGS

Bottles, K. 2000. "Leading in a Chaotic Health Care Environment." *Physician Executive* (July–August): 132–36.

Collins, J. 2004. "Defining Superior Leadership for the Next Generation." *Management Quarterly* 45 (3): 16–25.

Kouzes, J. M., and B. Z. Posner. 2004. "A Prescription for Leading in Cynical Times." *Ivey Business Journal* 68 (6): 1–7.

Romano, M. 2004. "Ready or not. Talented, High-Achieving Physicians Often Come Up Short in the Skills and Other Attributes Needed to Excel as CEO." *Modern Healthcare* 34 (17): 26–28.

CHAPTER 2

The Values-Based Definition

Dr. Malcolm Learned opened his health administration lecture with the question, "What is leadership?" Students offered the following responses:

- Getting groups of people to follow you.
- Using power appropriately to meet organizational objectives.
- The process of uniting individuals into groups to serve a vision or a mission.
- In the past, leadership was all about power, but today it is about influence.
- Understanding the global purpose of an organization, and giving direction to subordinates to ensure their work is serving that purpose.
- It stands for the position and the activity of making change and moving toward a goal.
- Leadership comes down to having interpersonal skills, and it really is something that you are born with. Some people are just leaders, and others are just followers.
- Using a set of skills to make improvements in society or in organizations.
- Getting results. In instances when the leader abuses his or her power, the results may not be good. But in other cases, the results are beneficial to all those concerned.

- Although it may not be politically correct to say, leadership is all about power. This power can be used to coerce people into doing things they would not do otherwise.

Dr. Learned closed the discussion by asking, "If we all have different definitions, how can we study leadership, and how can we improve ourselves as leaders?"

LEADERSHIP IS ONE of the most discussed and ultimately the most misunderstood concepts in management. Is it an art, a science, or both? Is leadership defined by the act, the process, or the skill? Is a person a leader because she is in charge of moving a team from Point A to Point B? Is someone a leader because he has followers? What is the mark of a good leader, and does it matter how a leader achieves greatness?

As an executive search consultant, I have noticed that "you know what I mean" is one of the most repeated phrases during my discussions with employers about what qualities they are looking for in a leader. Although employers offer their favorite general descriptors of a qualified leader—for example, "outstanding"; has "integrity and high energy"; and is "a people person, a team player, and results oriented"—they are hard-pressed to provide specific details. As a result, these employers resort to replying with "you know what I mean." After all the publications, seminars, speeches, and casual banter about leadership, not many senior managers can articulate a comprehensive definition of leadership.

Leadership is a living phenomenon; therefore, it is expected to shift shape according to its purpose and the demands of its followers and the environment. This adaptability to change is probably why a definition has been so elusive for many people.

This chapter presents several theories of leadership from the existing literature. In addition, the concept of personal values and its relationship with leadership is introduced.

LEADERSHIP PERSPECTIVES FROM THE LITERATURE

Leadership Versus Management Theory

In his book *A Force for Change,* John Kotter (1990) proposes that leadership is different from management because leadership is a process that focuses on making organizational changes, while management is primarily concerned with control and results. Although Kotter agrees that both responsibilities are important, he views leaders as the stimuli behind an organization's adoption of—and adaptation to—improved processes. As a result, his readers are convinced that being a leader is preferable to being a manager. The distinction is not strong enough, as all leaders manage and all managers lead.

Comprehensive Theory

Ralph Stogdill (1984) wrote what may be the most comprehensive treatise on leadership in *Stogdill's Handbook of Leadership.* In the book, Stogdill argues that leadership is any of the following:

- A focus of team processes
- Personality and its effects
- The art of inducing compliance
- The exercise of influence
- An act that results in others acting or responding in a shared direction
- A form of persuasion
- A power relation
- An instrument of goal achievement
- An emerging effect of interaction
- A differentiated role
- The initiation of structure

Furthermore, he believes that interaction between members of a team occurs when one team member modifies the motivation or competencies of others in the team. Leaders are "agents of change, persons whose acts affect other people more than other people's acts affect them" (Stogdill 1984).

This comprehensive catalog of definitions serves as a checklist, pointing leaders to areas for improvement. Although the comprehensive theory explains the technical aspects of leadership, it ignores the art and the spiritual side. Doing so makes leadership seem mechanical.

Competency-Based Leadership Theory

The various definitions under the comprehensive theory support the view that leadership is enabled by a set of competencies. The competency theory, which has gained a significant following in the last decade, suggests that leaders must show knowledge, skills, and abilities in several areas, such as communications and business. Competency-based leadership also means that the key competencies required for specific roles within a corporate culture are identified and prioritized.

For example, a chief financial officer will require different competencies than a chief medical officer. And a more formal, structured organization will dictate the need for different competencies than will a more laid-back environment. In *Exceptional Leadership,* coauthor Andrew Garman and I (2006, xvi) contend that the competency theory leads to "a better understanding of the key qualities that drive highly effective leadership."

The Institute of Medicine's (2003) report *Health Professions Education: A Bridge to Quality* gave impetus to the competency movement in healthcare. The report observes the insufficient number of tools for assessing the proficiency of healthcare professionals and suggests a set of core competencies designed to improve quality of care. Additionally, the Healthcare Leadership

Alliance—a collaboration among five healthcare professional associations—issued a competency tool with 300 competencies (for more information, see www.healthcareleadershipalliance.org). In the last several years, many other competency frameworks have been developed for both healthcare management practice and education (Stefl 2008).

Values contain a judgmental element in that they carry an individual's ideas as to what is right, good, or desirable.

—**Stephen Robbins (2005)**

By providing specific examples, the competency theory enables leaders to "see" the behaviors ideal for competent leadership. For instance, the traits/competencies of an effective communicator are not merely listed but also explained. Moreover, the competency approach promotes the development and use of indicators that can measure the strength or weakness of a given competency.

Because any competency model includes at least 80 competencies, it becomes a challenge to pick out the competencies critical for effective leadership. The book *Exceptional Leadership* lays out the 16 key competencies that distinguish great leadership from good leadership.

Process Theory

In the book *Organizational Behavior*, authors Robert Kreitner and Angelo Kinicki (1998) describe leadership as "a social influence process in which the leader seeks the voluntary participation of subordinates in an effort to reach organizational goals."

This definition is true in three ways:

1. Leadership is a process because it takes place over a period of time, with a beginning and an end. Usually, the end is the point when leadership's effectiveness may be ascertained.
2. Leadership does not mean intimidation of followers into participation. Some healthcare "leaders" coerce "volunteers" to help them accomplish goals, but this technique is never acceptable and is highly unethical.

3. Leadership moves toward achievement or is progress driven, which is another symbol of effectiveness.

Contingency Theory

In the contingency perspective, all leadership behaviors are dependent on three primary variables:

1. Leader
2. Followers
3. Situation

This theory argues that different types of leaders are needed for different types of people and situations. As Hughes, Ginnett, and Curphy (2009) explain: In contingency leadership, "leader effectiveness is primarily determined by selecting the right kind of leader for a certain situation or changing the situation to fit the particular leader's style."

Simply, this school of thought purports that leaders must have versatility and must be adaptable to various types of followers, organizations, and occurrences. It has great merit and is one of the most validated theories of leadership.

VALUES-DRIVEN LEADERSHIP

I contend that

1. Leadership is both inherent and learned.
2. Leadership values and skills are interrelated. One cannot exist without the other.

Numerous studies suggest that many leadership skills and traits are the result of heredity (Hughes, Ginnett, and Curphy 2009). In this vein, so-called born leaders tend to develop certain values and exhibit strong leadership characteristics and skills early in life. Those who are not born leaders, on the other hand, must cultivate these values to enhance their leadership capabilities, a belief that many managers, executives, and consultants—including me—hold.

What definitive characteristic differentiates strong leaders from weak leaders? What trait drives the behavior of effective leaders? What quality do successful leaders possess that average leaders do not have? The only answer is having the appropriate leadership values.

What Are Values?

Values are ingrained principles that guide behaviors and thoughts. They are formed early in life and develop with experiences, and they usually do not change much during a lifetime. As a moral framework, values help an individual analyze options, make decisions during times of stress, and rise above difficult or unexpected situations. Values are not necessarily all positive, however. Exhibit 2.1 provides

Exhibit 2.1 The Iceberg Analogy of Leadership Values

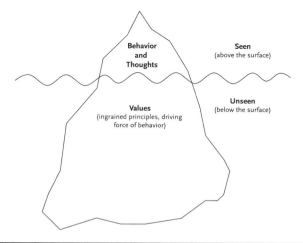

an analogy for understanding how values are connected with and drive behaviors and thoughts.

Everyone has values, but those values differ from person to person. Some people have values that affect their leadership effectiveness. For example, Leader A values being around other people, while Leader B values being alone. Because Leader A spends time with others, she is more exposed to others' ideas and practices. She can learn from this exposure and, in the process, develop an appreciation for and openness to different experiences. Leader B's values, on the other hand, may not be as conducive to leadership improvement because he is isolated from the opinions and experiences of others. The real advantage of values depends on the degree to which a person allows these values to influence her development.

Personal and Team Values

Personal values affect how a leader perceives and is perceived by others. If leadership is a "social influence process," as Kreitner and Kinicki (1998) suggest, then values can make an impact—negatively or positively—on this process. A leader is most influential when his followers know what he stands for because followers are clear on whether or not they can relate to the leader's ideals. This concept is illustrated at every election campaign, as candidates lay out their personal beliefs in hopes of gaining supporters. The same can be said of chief executive officers when they seek buy-in from organizational stakeholders.

In addition, personal values guide the interactions between a leader and her followers, serving as the "fluid" of the social interchange. Under the contingency theory, in which a leader considers all variables before making a decision and going forward, an effective leader relies on her values to steer her toward the most appropriate action.

Team values are the collective rights and wrongs of a group. These values guide the behavior, decisions, and actions of team members. They also set the standards for how members interact with each other and work together, given that each member holds differing personal values that could cause conflicts in the group. In an organization, team values are often, if not always, tied to the mission of the enterprise. For example, if the mission is "to serve those in need, regardless of their ability to pay," the team values will likely include community service, respect for diversity, accountability, and open communication, not pursuit of profits or one-upmanship.

Both personal and team values contribute to leadership effectiveness. Exhibit 2.2 provides a distinction between these two types of values.

Impact of Values

Values enable leaders to go through the stages in leadership growth. Following is a description of each stage (also see Exhibit 2.3).

Exhibit 2.2 Personal Values Versus Team Values

Personal Values	Team Values
How a leader perceives and is perceived by other people	How a group behaves, performs tasks, and achieves goals / How members interact with one another

Exhibit 2.3 The Learning and Mastery Process

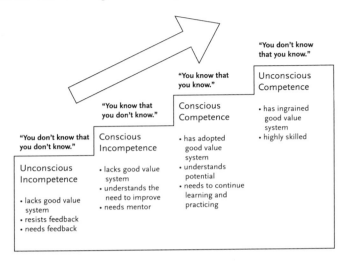

Unconscious Incompetence

"You don't know that you don't know." This is the most difficult stage for many leaders because they are unaware of their own mistakes and flaws. Often, they work in successful organizations and do not even consider that problems with their leadership skills might exist. Leaders who are most likely at this level are those who have not started to develop appropriate leadership values or may be highly resistant to the input and feedback of others. As a result, they need training and awareness to enhance their self-understanding.

Conscious Incompetence

"You know that you don't know." Although this stage is the most important step toward learning, it can be the most challenging because sometimes you have to lose your job before you realize that your performance needs work. For others, this realization is a gradual process and may come as the result of the influence of a strong mentor or coach and a sincere desire to grow and improve.

Conscious Competence

"You know that you know." Although this stage comprises leaders who are neither born nor strong, this is when they start developing and honing their potential. Leaders at this stage work very hard to put into practice appropriate skills, but they sometimes fail because the skills are not part of their natural thinking habits yet.

> We need authentic leaders, people of the highest integrity, committed to building enduring organizations. We need leaders who have a deep sense of purpose and are true to their core values.
>
> —Bill George (2003)

Unconscious Competence

"You don't know that you know." This is the ultimate stage of leadership development because the activities here flow smoothly with neither great force nor hesitation. Leaders at this level seem to be naturals at their trade. This is truly descriptive of a "born leader."

CONCLUSION

Developing an operative definition of leadership is necessary for growth, so leaders must increase their knowledge and awareness by reading more books on the topic and exploring more and various approaches to leadership. Leaders should personalize these definitions and theories to fit their own milieu and quest for self-improvement.

Defining and evaluating one's leadership skills are the first steps toward improvement. Individuals should interact with other leaders to discuss their strategies. Finally, they should observe their own impact within the organization.

Allowing positive values to be a primary influencer enables leaders to better judge their own style. Parts II and III of this book identify the values that guide leaders and team members. See Appendix A for a professional and personal values assessment tool.

* What do I value? Do these values assist or hinder my leadership activities?
* Are my behaviors guided by personal principles?
* What personal values of mine may conflict with my role and responsibilities as a leader?
* Have I written a narrative describing my leadership style? Did I do it to impress a search consultant or a potential employer, or did I do it to evaluate my strengths and weaknesses?
* What is my definition of leadership?
* List several successful healthcare leaders. What traits do they have in common? What values do they share?
* Do I view leadership as an act, a process, or a skill? After reading Chapter 2, how will my answer to this question differ?

SUGGESTED READINGS

Alexander, C., D. Campbell, J. Leiferman, G. Mabey, S. Marken, C. Myers, A. Pengra, T. Reyburn-Orne, T. S. Sundem, and C. Zwingman-Bagley. 2003. "Quality Improvement Processes in Growing a Service Line." *Nursing Administration Quarterly* 27 (4): 297–306.

Brown, M. E., and L. K. Treviño. 2006. "Socialized Charismatic Leadership, Values Congruence, and Deviance in Work Groups." *Journal of Applied Psychology* 91 (4): 954–62.

Carmeli, A., and M. Y. Halevi. 2009. "How Top Management Team Behavioral Integration and Behavioral Complexity Enable Organizational Ambidexterity: The Moderating Role of Contextual Ambidexterity." *Leadership Quarterly* 20 (2): 207–18.

Clark, L. 2008. "Clinical Leadership: Values, Beliefs and Vision." *Nursing Management* 15 (7): 30–35.

Dye, C. F., and A. N. Garman. 2006. *Exceptional Leadership: 16 Critical Competencies for Healthcare Leaders.* Chicago: Health Administration Press.

Garman, A. N., and M. Johnson. 2006. "Leadership Competencies: An Introduction." *Journal of Healthcare Management* 51 (1): 13–17.

Hughes, R. L., R. C. Ginnett, and G. J. Curphy. 2009. *Leadership: Enhancing the Lesson of Experience,* 6th edition. Columbus, OH: McGraw-Hill/Irwin.

Karp, T., and T. I. Tveteraas Helgø. 2009. "Reality Revisited: Leading People in Chaotic Change." *Journal of Management Development* 28 (2): 81–93.

Miles, R. E. 2007. "Innovation and Leadership Values." *California Management Review* 50 (1): 192–201.

Reave, L. 2005. "Spiritual Values and Practices Related to Leadership Effectiveness." *Leadership Quarterly* 16 (5): 655–87.

Scanland, W., and D. Pepper. 1978. "The Rationale and Methodology for Development of a Competency Based Leadership Education and Training Program in the Navy." Paper presented at the Annual Meeting of the American Educational Research Association, March 27–31, Toronto, Canada. [Online information; retrieved 11/20/09.] www.eric.ed.gov/ERICWebPortal/custom/portlets/recordDetails/detailmini.jsp?_nfpb=true&_&ERICExtSearch_SearchValue_0=ED154147&ERICExtSearch_SearchType_0=no&accno=ED154147.

Souba, W. W., and D. V. Day. 2006. "Leadership Values in Academic Medicine." *Academic Medicine: Journal of the Association of American Medical Colleges* 81 (1): 20–26.

Souba, W. W., D. Mauger, and D. V. Day. 2007. "Does Agreement on Institutional Values and Leadership Issues Between Deans and Surgery Chairs Predict Their Institutions' Performance?" *Academic Medicine: Journal of the Association of American Medical Colleges* 82 (3): 272–80.

Stanley, D. 2008. "Congruent Leadership: Values in Action." *Journal of Nursing Management* 16 (5): 519–24.

Yukl, G. 2010. *Leadership in Organizations,* 7th edition. Upper Saddle River, NJ: Prentice-Hall.

Case and Exercise

Case 2.1

Three health system vice presidents (VPs) are discussing leadership over lunch. The first VP says, "Leadership is completely about relationships. It is about how you work with people and how you get to know them as individuals." The second VP replies, "I agree that people are important, but you can have a lot of happy people and not achieve any goals. That is not leadership in my book." The third VP comments, "You both have good points, but you are really missing the key of leadership—that is vision. A lot of what you are talking about is management. Leadership is developing a vision and getting the organization moving toward that vision."

You join these three VPs at the table, and they ask for your thoughts on this issue.

Questions
1. Describe in detail how each VP's argument is right and wrong.
2. How might their differing viewpoints be melded together to provide a comprehensive and accurate description of leadership?

Exercise 2.1
Following are the major leadership theories in existence today, including their creators (in parentheses):

- "Great Man" theory (Mortimer Adler)
- Trait theory (Ralph Stogdill)
- Contingency theory (Fred Fiedler)
- Situational theories (Paul Hersey and Ken Blanchard)
- Behavioral theories (Robert Blake and Jane Mouton)
- Participative theories (Kurt Lewin, Rensis Likert)
- Transactional leadership (Max Weber and Bernard Bass)
- Transformational leadership (James McGregor Burns and Bernard Bass)
- Emotional intelligence (Daniel Goleman)

Take two of the major theories listed above and study them using the following framework:

1. Describe the theory in detail.
2. Explain how the theory can be applied in a work setting.
3. List one or two major limitations of the theory.

CHAPTER 3

The Senior Leader Challenge

THE TEMPERATURE OF the head is often a good indicator of the temperature of the body. This truism applies to healthcare organizations as well. Therefore, to gauge the health of a healthcare system, it is imperative to examine the wellness of its head—the senior leaders. Because the senior leadership team functions as the primary decision makers and establishes the mission, vision, values, culture, and practices of an organization, it sets the tone and pace for organizational change and improvement.

The leadership challenges in healthcare have been similar for many years, focusing on finance and quality. However, some of these issues have become more critical and new ones have surfaced, as mentioned in Chapter 1. Following are specific challenges in the last five years:

- Responding to community needs and appropriately reporting community benefits
- Recruiting and retaining staff amid growing labor shortages and ongoing retirements
- Dealing with increased unionization and staffing mandates
- Competing in a global healthcare market
- Managing ethically and with transparency
- Ensuring patient privacy and securing medical records

- Covering the uninsured and underinsured
- Easing emergency department overcrowding
- Creating succession and transition plans
- Finding new sources of revenue in a recession
- Complying with ever-changing regulations
- Involving patients and families in a consumer-driven market
- Implementing information technology systems

Exhibit 3.1 defines these and other issues.

This chapter gives voice to senior leaders' main concerns—be they internal or external to their organizations and the industry. The intent here is to raise awareness that values-driven leaders have an advantage over these seemingly insurmountable challenges.

Exhibit 3.1 Pressures on Healthcare Leaders

Quality of care and patient safety. The Institute of Medicine's (2000, 2001) reports *To Err Is Human* and *Crossing the Quality Chasm* have galvanized national efforts to improve the quality of care and reduce patient errors. Many healthcare organizations have participated in this movement—notably the initiatives by the Institute for Healthcare Improvement (see www.ihi.org).

Waste and errors. Six Sigma and Lean Management theories are two of the outside-industry methods that reduce waste and errors in healthcare.

Reimbursement system. The current system is fragmented, with multiple payers, differing requirements, and complex coding and charges. Reimbursement has declined, forcing organizations to shift costs to cover expenses.

Community benefit. Not-for-profit hospitals and health systems must prove they provide community benefit. The Centers for Medicare &

(continued)

(continued)

Medicaid Services released a new form in 2008 that requires a more detailed accounting of this public service.

Recruitment and succession planning. Many healthcare workers, including executives, are retiring or due to retire in several years. This problem is compounded by labor shortages and the aging of the population, which will increase the demands on already overworked and understaffed healthcare organizations. Recruitment, retention, and succession planning are just a few of the human resource pressures on senior leaders.

Organizational structure. With the increased number of multihospital/integrated systems and their corresponding array of legal entities, lines of authority and expectations are not as clear.

Diversity. The U.S. population has continually become more diverse, yet healthcare leadership has been slow to reflect this change.

Ethics. The public, industry watchdogs, and legislators continue to demand greater transparency and more accountability in healthcare delivery and management.

Leadership development. The need for leadership development has never been greater. Now is the time to encourage continuous learning.

ORGANIZATIONAL FACTORS

Now more than ever, senior leaders need to depend on their strong values to effectively manage their hospitals and health systems. One of the reasons chaos sometimes arises is that senior leaders fail to anticipate, manage through, and rise above the inevitable changes in the industry. In fairness to leaders, however, organizational factors do exist that can impede their performance and can exacerbate the effects of the current leadership challenges. These factors are described in this section.

Complex Organizational Structure

Mergers, acquisitions, alliances, affiliations, coalitions, federations, and other types of partnerships reinvented how healthcare services are delivered, paid for, and measured. This redesign created the need for more managers to oversee the quality and flow of even more services. Ultimately, a complex network of managers with various titles was born, making up a vast structural maze.

Many hospitals have become health systems, and to flourish or at least survive in a competitive market, these facilities have adopted multiple business lines. Often, this expansion has created a schism between leaders who are involved in only external transactions (e.g., physician practice acquisitions, alliances, new business lines) and those who oversee day-to-day operations.

Rapid growth has also diversified the composition and enlarged the size of the typical senior leadership team. As a result, the personal and professional camaraderie that used to bind senior leaders is almost extinct, and the meetings have become too large for intimate and goal-driven interaction. Some teams convene as many as 20 to 30 people. As discussed later in this chapter, both research and common sense prove that a team this large cannot be effective.

Haphazard Executive Search Process

Little preparation or forethought is given to the executive hiring process; organizations usually just jump in to start recruitment. Although employers are clear on their intentions to search extensively and select the best candidate, they are vague on the actual execution of this plan. This type of hiring may also be classified as "start and stop," whereby the organization moves quickly to advertise the vacancy or contracts with a search firm, then pauses the process for an indefinite period, and then slowly re-enters it before getting back on track. Here, the message seems to be that the employer has bigger priorities, forcing it to delay the recruitment process.

Poor preparation causes executive hiring decisions to be made too subjectively or on "gut feeling," not based on the organization's true needs or the position's expectations and qualifications. With gut-feeling hiring, many executive search processes become an endurance test for those involved, focusing almost exclusively on interpersonal style and fit. The unfortunate result is sometimes the selection of a leader who has inadequate leadership competencies (see Chapter 2) and knowledge of the industry.

> Complacency is a deadly affliction for people and organizations, and healthcare organizations are not immune.
>
> —Jeff Goldsmith (1998)

Litigious Environment

Many challenges faced by leaders today are new. Because these leaders have had no prior knowledge of or experience with the matters at hand, their decisions are often based on best guesses, a risky and potentially fatal move.

The legal ramifications of some of these issues further complicate decision-making processes. For example, a hospital could be sued for failing to secure proper consent from a patient or his guardian; likewise, a health system could find itself a defendant in a medical malpractice suit (see Showalter 2008 for a closer look at these healthcare-related cases). With the continued growth of systems and consolidations, antitrust considerations become important. One chief executive officer (CEO) remarks that the "mission too often takes the back seat to legal maneuvering."

Fast Pace of Change

The traditional mind-set in healthcare is to follow predictable, tried processes; therefore, many of its leaders are reluctant to adopt innovative or even alternative strategies or methods of operation. The proliferation of information on the Internet and the fast speed at which this information can be accessed encourage leaders to change with the times and make fast decisions. In fact, leaders who are unable to function in a modern, technological world are seen as a big liability because they fail to anticipate and thus capitalize on innovation and other advances. On the other hand, leaders who are "linked in" are said to be informed, headed in the right direction, and even ahead of the competition.

Those characterizations may be right. However, there is a casualty in this fast-moving trend: The quality of the decisions suffers because leaders do not have enough time to consult with each other or to reflect on the implications of their decisions. A CEO from the Midwest admits that her board is often frustrated with the number and speed of significant decisions that her team has to make without thoughtful deliberation.

Decision making without proper analysis is prevalent in any industry; it is a product of the rapidly transforming world, with or without the availability of the Internet, mobile devices, and other technology-based media. A leader's strong values can help when both time and information are limited but demands are endless.

Lack of Time

If the ability to stop time could be bottled and sold, it would sell out even before the cap is twisted closed. Some of its first buyers would certainly be senior leaders and their team members. Lack of time (specifically, the constant pressure to produce/decide within a limited time) has resulted in burnout and stress.

In addition, lack of time has led to the following:

1. *Communication problems.* Because the meeting agenda is filled with so many pressing issues, not all members of the leadership team can convey their thoughts. Even those who have the

opportunity to do so cannot properly elaborate on their ideas. On the other hand, some leaders may counter that so much time is spent on meeting minutiae that less time is appropriated for actual strategy evaluation.

2. *Less interaction among senior leaders.* Frontline managers spend more time working together than do senior leaders. Many senior teams come together only occasionally, and thus they are less familiar and friendly with each other. At this level, personal and professional conflicts tend to exist more and can be more volatile. Capricious members use insider knowledge to intimidate and subdue opposing members. Knowledge is frequently withheld.

3. *Reliance on e-mail.* Time-strapped leaders share information and consult about decisions through e-mail. While this method is more efficient than a phone call, it prevents the proper "airing out" of issues and may overlook the input of stakeholders who are not privy to the e-mail sequence.

Lack of Shared Vision

Goals are achievable only when everyone on a team is deeply committed to them. Unfortunately, many senior leaders move in opposite directions, harbor personal agendas, and have little personal or professional compatibility with colleagues. While some leaders focus on external business development activities, others commit to managing acute care outcomes. Goals such as improving health system performance or enhancing quality and patient safety are more abstract than the goals set out by lower-level management teams within the organization. The threat of losing their jobs, which is always a possibility, especially in a financially difficult time, can turn some leaders into fierce competitors and has created a negative political landscape.

CONCLUSION

One of the most important characteristics of strong leaders is the ability to objectively analyze their performance and their impact on the organization. Part IV of this book provides various assessment tools. Consider the concepts in this chapter and apply them to your organization.

Self-Evaluation Questions

* How influential is the senior leadership team in my organization?
* Does the frequent turnover among senior leadership team members create a serious, negative effect on the team's effectiveness? Why?

Exercises

Exercise 3.1

Question: Which group has the greater ability to change an organization—senior leaders or middle managers?

Viewpoint: Senior leaders have far more impact and ability to change an organization for several reasons. First, they create and interpret organizational policies. Second, they assess the environment and develop strategy. Third, they control the budget and make the ultimate decisions regarding executive hires. Fourth, they have better insight into environmental trends than do middle managers. Last, their span of control is greater, and they work closely with the board.

Do you agree with this viewpoint? Why? Why not? What points do you think are untrue of today's senior leaders?

Exercise 3.2

The layers of hierarchy between a senior leader and a middle manager continue to peel off in many industries, including healthcare. Using information gleaned from the Internet along the themes listed below, contrast the role and activities of a senior leader with that of a middle manager. If possible, interview a senior leader and a middle manager.

Questions

1. What are the typical responsibilities of a senior leader?
2. What are the typical responsibilities of a middle manager?
3. How is a senior leader rewarded and recognized? How do these acknowledgments differ from those received by a middle manager?

Suggested Readings for This Exercise

- Henri Fayol's span of control theory. This theory may be found in any organizational behavior textbook.
- Peter Drucker's *The Practice of Management*. See www.allbusiness.com/management/412518-1.html
- Amy McCutcheon and Ruth Anne Campbell's "Leadership, Span of Control, Turnover, Staff & Patient Satisfaction." See http://stti.confex.com/stti/inrc16/techprogram/paper_23430.htm. This article discusses the relationship among span of control, employee turnover, and patient satisfaction.

PART II

PERSONAL VALUES

CHAPTER 4

Respect in Stewardship

On the eve of the 2009 healthcare reform vote, John George, a system CEO, and Julia Garrison, a vice president, discuss the state of the healthcare industry.

Julia: John, how has healthcare changed since you first entered it in the 1970s? It seems that the field and its workers are not as respected today.

John: Back then, many of us saw healthcare management as a calling. We wanted to serve people, to make a difference. Now too many people go into it as if it is just another career.

Julia: I disagree. Most of us new administrators are still service oriented. The problem is healthcare leaders have been viewed as villains, even though we do a lot, directly and indirectly, to improve the health and lives of our patients and our workers. Do you think the old days of the command-and-control healthcare CEO may have something to do with this negative public perception?

John: Perhaps you are right, although I wouldn't say the autocratic leader is now a relic of the past. Unfortunately, they still exist, and they certainly harm the reputation of all healthcare administrators. Here is my challenge to you: Talk with your colleagues, do some research, and make a recommendation about how to effect a sea change in management. We'll discuss your findings, and we'll see how we can implement changes in our own backyard, so to speak.

> Stewardship begins with the willingness to be accountable for some larger body than ourselves—an organization, a community. Stewardship springs from a set of beliefs about reforming organizations that affirms our choice for service over the pursuit of self-interest.
>
> —Peter Block (1993)

IF LEADERSHIP IS a journey, then respect for constituents is its fuel. Without respect, leadership is a farcical, stagnant voyage. Respect is the value that multiplies the desire of both the leader and follower to work harder and deliver consistently excellent performance.

Stewardship, or leadership, is traditionally perceived as a prestigious position filled by influential people whose main role is to give orders and impose inflexible rules. This misconception may not be as prevalent now because more leaders have become aware that autocratic management begets only few and uneasy followers. Society frequently rejects selfish stewardship. This type of behavior repeatedly leads to entitlement, greed, and other peccadilloes, as has been frequently reported in the media in the past decade. As a result, many Americans distrust and are cynical about the C-suite in all industries, as illustrated by the opening vignette.

Respect for self and others is the nucleus of all activities, especially in management. It is a value that enables leaders to restrain ego, admit mistakes, pay attention, care about and honor others, keep an open mind, give credit or compliments, and ask for help or insight. Stewards must return to this basic value to regain trust and to amplify their effectiveness. Although the task is daunting, it is a worthwhile undertaking.

For many years now, I have spoken and written about the protocols of leadership (see Dye 2000, for example). These protocols are the often unwritten behavioral rules society and organizations expect from their stewards. These generally accepted standards of behavior cannot possibly cover all situations faced by an executive, but they share a common element: respect.

This chapter makes a distinction between self-esteem and self-centeredness, two opposing forces in management style. While self-esteem boosts the persuasiveness of a leader, self-centeredness undermines this power altogether. In addition, the chapter also provides several approaches for showing and gaining respect (see Exhibit 4.1).

SELF-ESTEEM VERSUS SELF-CENTEREDNESS

Self-esteem is an individual's respect for her own convictions, actions, imperfections, and abilities. Without self-esteem, a person is not mentally healthy; does not function well under pressure; cannot accept or give compliments and criticism; and tends to be egotistical, controlling, and in constant need of affirmation.

Self-centeredness, on the other hand, is an individual's overly favorable sense of his own abilities, views, decisions, and needs. A self-centered person is arrogant, insecure (yet feels superior), and a nuisance (if not harmful) in any social or professional setting.

Stewards who have low self-esteem but are highly self-centered

- do not respect or trust others;
- alienate others with a domineering attitude;

Exhibit 4.1 Four Ways to Show Respect for Others

1. Give compliments, be courteous, and show good manners and pleasant deportment to show that you appreciate and honor the efforts that others bring to the organization.
2. Learn the strength of collective action through the cooperative work of teams.
3. Ask and listen to what others value, need, and expect.
4. Participate in others' activities to show you care about their interests.

- are exasperating because they seek/demand so much approval;
- cause unnecessary work and waste time; and
- engender disloyalty, stress, and fear.

Exhibit 4.2 contrasts self-esteem with self-centeredness.

THE CONCEPT IN PRACTICE

Following are some ways a steward can show respect in various facets of her position.

Become a Collaborator

Collaboration is a partnership among people who have shared goals but distinct strategies or priorities. The reasons for collaboration are varied, including to expedite achievement of results; combine expertise, experience, and resources; minimize or prevent mistakes and waste in effort, time, and money; and produce a better product.

Exhibit 4.2 Contrast Between Self-Esteem and Self-Centeredness

Self-Esteem		Self-Centeredness
Respect for self	vs.	Overly favorable concept of self
Accepts and gives compliments and criticism gracefully	vs.	Demands constant approval while being unduly critical
Collaborates and cooperates with others	vs.	Alienates others with an arrogant approach
Stays efficient by relying on colleagues for aid	vs.	Doubts others, creating unnecessary work
Cultivates an inclusive, team-oriented atmosphere	vs.	Fosters disloyalty and suspicion in the workplace

Leaders who become good collaborators learn to

- hold judgment until all the variables and others' opinions have been presented;
- listen actively;
- reflect before responding; and
- ask questions to understand, not to cast doubt.

Exhibit 4.3 is a basic guide to effective collaboration.

Senior leaders must push other executives to seek collaborations with those in lower-level positions. Why is this necessary? Because collaboration is about equal exchange of ideas, not a privileged activity of those at the top of the organizational hierarchy. An interoffice collaboration that includes multilevel partners is a sign that the stewards respect the insight and contributions of all employees.

Exhibit 4.3 Key Requirements of Effective Collaboration

Common desired outcome. The collaboration must offer a reciprocal benefit to all partners or participants. The stakeholders must believe they are getting something good in return for their efforts and the end product improves the current situation.

Shared responsibility. The driving force of a true collaboration is shared responsibility—from decision making to implementation to monitoring and assessment. All members of the partnership, not just its leaders, must be able to voice their concerns, opinions, and questions. Consensus must be reached at all times. Responsibility for failure or negative consequences must also be shared by all involved.

Support. In a collaborative situation, parties to the process support each other's right to express ideas and suggestions. When a decision is made to move forward, all stakeholders support the conclusion.

(continued)

(continued)

Clear objective. The group must have a clear understanding of the collaboration's purpose or goal.

Trust. Trust is built when all partners commit to be transparent and share information. A willingness to admit mistakes also helps in this regard.

Open communication. Suspending judgment, not assigning blame, active listening, being interested and inquisitive, and checking in or following up promote open communication among collaborators.

Celebration. Gains and accomplishments must be celebrated. Doing so encourages participants.

Be Aware of Others' Definition of Respect

Respect means different things to different people. For example, Person A may perceive respect when he is asked for his opinion, while Person B may feel respected if she is empowered to make an important decision.

For many people, the level of respect they give or demand depends on superficial attributes, such as job title. Unfortunately, respect for those who clean the facilities, for example, seems nonexistent in many industries. Likewise, professors and students alike may not show as much respect for their university's security personnel or cafeteria staff. In clinical practice, physicians are traditionally more respected than nurses or allied health professionals. In management, executives garner more respect than receptionists and other frontline employees.

A good steward understands these dynamics and recognizes everyone's human dignity and basic need for respect. When asked how he shows respect, a successful CEO says, "I hire the very best people

> Being in a position to exercise power over other people may be satisfying for a little while, but never in the long run. Ultimately it leaves you lonely. You command, and you receive fear and obedience in return, and what emotionally healthy person can live on a diet of fear and obedience?
>
> —Harold S. Kushner (1986)

I can find, and then I show them the respect they are due by staying out of their way and letting them do their jobs." Another high-performing CEO reveals, "All of my executive team members think and act like each is my COO [chief operations officer]—and most importantly, they make most of their decisions without my involvement." These two quotes exemplify how leaders can show respect by empowering their staff.

Establish a Feedback System

The best feedback systems are those that provide constant, unfiltered, direct feedback and, when necessary, criticism. Feedback should be given on an ongoing basis and should be informal. The recipient of the feedback should be given an opportunity to respond, ask questions, or simply confirm his understanding.

In the book *Giving and Receiving Performance Feedback*, author Peter Garber (2004) indicates that in most organizations, it has become increasingly rare that true open dialogue occurs in traditional performance evaluation sessions. Executives' interactions are more often than not held in the C-suite, a setting that can intimidate most people. The fact that the leaders giving the evaluation have the power to hire and fire adds to the tension. As a result of these trappings, stewards may be less skilled at evaluating their direct reports and vice versa (Garman and Dye 2009).

Seeking and receiving feedback is a sign of respect, communicating that others' opinions are valued. When leaders interact with staff regularly, they appear accessible and are better informed.

> Leaders are best when people barely know they exist, not so good when people obey and acclaim them, worse when people despise them. But of good leaders, who talk little, when their work is finished, their aim fulfilled, the others will say 'We did this ourselves.'
>
> —Lao Tzu

Be Genuine

Genuineness is also referred to as "authentic presence." It can be conveyed by being visibly involved in organizational activities and showing a vested interest in others' work without being intrusive and pretentious. The unspoken message here is "We are in this together."

Many CEOs practice Management by Walking Around (MBWA), a popular strategy among stewards. MBWA's primary purpose is to witness the effectiveness or ineffectiveness of various services and, by extension, those who perform the work. Although MBWA provides great insight and breeds familiarity, it should be carefully managed to ensure that employees believe the approach is sincere.

In Catholic hospitals, nuns (many of them top administrators) traditionally were known to be extraordinary influencers because they were frequently visible and consistently approachable. Physicians tend to gravitate toward physician leaders because they relate to these executives and believe they can better represent their needs, understand their concerns, and defend their demands. This is even more true for the physician leaders who still maintain some amount of clinical practice.

Give Credit and Acknowledge Accomplishments

The mark of a great leader is his ability to stand back from the spotlight and publicly recognize someone else's excellent performance. This simple acknowledgment is one of the most powerful motivators, much quieter than a standing ovation but more valuable than money.

Offer Help or Coaching

Many leaders study coaching to enhance their abilities to evaluate, constructively criticize, and assist their staff's performance. By helping staff develop, the leader is saying: "I admire and respect your work so much that I want to invest in your growth and accomplishments."

Be Self-Aware

Leaders must be able to look inward to discover their strengths, weaknesses, goals, and impetus. Creativity often springs from being self-aware. In *Exceptional Leadership*, a well-cultivated self-awareness is named as one of the four key cornerstones in superb leadership (Dye and Garman 2006). This approach requires strong feedback mechanisms as well as a willingness to consider with an open mind the input received.

Take Responsibility for Mistakes and Apologize

This is often the most overlooked way of showing respect. Many leaders fail to realize that by simply owning up to their mistakes and apologizing, they are loudly proclaiming that they are penetrable, they are vincible, and they are human—hence, on the same level as others. What others hear when leaders say "I made a mistake and I'm sorry" is "I respect you, so I will not pretend or make you believe that what happened was your responsibility."

Learn the Principle of Affirmation

The word "affirm" comes from an ancient legal principle: the higher court must approve the decision of the lower court. In this parallel, stewards function as the higher court that affirms the work and contributions of their employees (the lower court). This principle serves as a powerful, positive message and a great motivator for better performance.

Positive affirmations are statements and behaviors that build others up and boost their confidence and sense of well-being. They serve to minimize the many negative distractions that occur in the workplace. The advice that leaders give in the workplace and the atmosphere created by leaders in an organization help to shape the attitude that others will have of that organization.

Show Appreciation

A note of congratulations, appreciation, or gratitude has always been a staple of good camaraderie. Many leaders still make time to handwrite notes, but this practice has declined as e-mails and phone calls have become more popular for their convenience and speed. Nevertheless, the idea is the same: A small token makes a big impression.

Show Enthusiasm

Some leaders may think that showing enthusiasm about an endeavor is inappropriate, unprofessional, or even silly. However, it has a positive effect on followers. Enthusiasm can energize people and boost loyalty to the undertaking.

Showing enthusiasm and support for the mission of the organization is also important because the rank and file model the behavior of their leaders. Employees can become cynical if they only hear but do not see their leaders' support of the mission.

Enthusiasm may also be expressed through attending or participating in employee events. Failure to make an appearance or embrace these events can drive a wedge between the C-suite and the front line, perpetuating the perception that senior leaders are only interested in activities that revolve around the power structure. As one executive's flippant remark expressed: "I really see no sense in serving hot dogs at the employee picnic. Let others handle that, and I'll handle my job."

CONCLUSION

Respectful stewardship may be common-sense knowledge to some leaders. However, it is surprisingly a novel concept to many others. Admittedly, it is hard to master and even harder to convince people to try, especially in an industry that is already overwhelmed with too many "must dos." But respect is not a temporary fix or trend; it is a fundamental value in all aspects of life.

✳   ✳   ✳

———— Self-Evaluation Questions ————

* What does respect mean to me?
* Can I respect others and still be accountable for their actions?
* Stewardship often sounds as if it has religious connotations. How do I define it?
* Do I have an appropriate feedback mechanism to assess how others view me?

SUGGESTED READINGS

Bono, J. E., and A. E. Colbert. 2005. "Understanding Responses to Multi-Source Feedback: The Role of Core Self-Evaluations." *Personnel Psychology* 58: 171–203.

Hiller, N. J., and D. C. Hambrick. 2005. "Conceptualizing Executive Hubris: The Role of (Hyper-) Core Self-Evaluations in Strategic Decision-Making." *Strategic Management Journal* 26: 297–319.

Cases

Case 4.1

Roberto Santiago has been CEO of St. James for the last three years. He was hired for his strategic visioning acumen, and he spends his time in meetings with board members, community leaders, and physicians. Recently, he led a successful strategic planning retreat, garnering him strong supporters from the board and medical staff.

Roberto has put Jane Robbins, the chief operations officer, in charge of running St. James's daily operations. Jane oversees the vice presidents and attends all staff meetings. During a monthly housekeeping meeting, Jane fielded questions from the housekeeping staff. One asked, "We never see Mr. Santiago. Does he not care what happens to us?"

How would you answer this question if you were Jane Robbins?

Case 4.2

Courtney Sample is the new hard-charging, tough-as-nails CEO of a system hospital. She is well-known for delivering great results, but sometimes at the expense of many. Previously, she executed a multiyear, multimillion-dollar turnaround of a bankrupt hospital, replacing the entire senior leadership team in the process.

Six months into her current position, Courtney is frustrated. She has not been able to finish a single project, and morale among her team is at an all-time low. Many of the employees and physicians are unfamiliar with her, and those who know her avoid eye contact. She scheduled an appointment with her long-time personal coach, Will Cheng, to seek his help. Will spent a day talking with Courtney's staff and then met with her over dinner.

Will: You intimidate your staff. They didn't even want to talk to me. They think you view them like tools, just there to get the job done.

Courtney: Isn't that what we all are anyway? Tools to get the job done?"

Questions
1. How can showing respect help Courtney out of this scenario? What can Will do and say to correct Courtney's misguided attitude?
2. How is the concept of respect a constant in *all* leadership settings? Consider the leader who states, "Sometimes, I want my followers to fear me." Is this ever appropriate?

CHAPTER 5

Ethics and Integrity

In a popular graduate health administration course, a well-known ethicist poses difficult questions to the students: "What makes a leader good? Successful? Effective? Was Adolf Hitler a good leader? How about Joseph Stalin? Saddam Hussein?"

A heated discussion ensues.

The professor turns to a topic specific to his students—ethics in healthcare management: "If a certain organizational change does not result in improvement or a benefit for all, can you call that leader and the undertaking ethical?"

Student A: First, you have to define what a leader is supposed to do. Then, you can determine the ethics from there.

Student B: It's all about the end result. Outcomes are important in healthcare; that's what we are here to do—help make positive changes for people.

Student C: I have a problem with the idea that something is ethical just because it benefits a great number of people. That shortchanges the role that values need to play in leadership. What about the minority number who are inevitably disadvantaged by the change? Don't they count? What about the leader who ignored her moral compass just so she could provide for the many?

Professor: Excellent responses! There are no easy answers in ethics, which is why it is important to have discussions about these issues.

> Leaders who do not behave ethically do not demonstrate true leadership.
>
> —J. M. Burns (1978)

As are other leadership values, ethics and integrity are interrelated. Ethics is a person's moral scope, and integrity is the person's capacity for staying within that moral scope. The general concept of both values is comprehensible, but their true meaning is elusive.

This chapter explores the tandem nature of ethics and integrity. It provides a guide for leaders on how to practice ethical behavior within the constructs of daily operation. While the vignette presents both a macro and a micro view of ethics, this chapter focuses primarily on leaders' daily activities.

DEFINING INTEGRITY

Practically all leaders believe they possess high integrity. However, when asked to name other leaders who have integrity, many demur by saying "integrity is hard to define." Why the contradiction? Two reasons are plausible.

First, many definitions for integrity exist, but none is universal. According to the *Merriam-Webster's Collegiate Dictionary,* 11th edition, integrity is "the quality or state of being complete or undivided." To some people, the word could mean absolute honesty, while to others, it is a high degree of genuineness. My definition is the quality that allows a person to differentiate right from wrong. Each definition almost always reflects a person's sensibility (e.g., moral compass, bias, expectation). Thus, applying it to others can be a difficult proposition.

Second, our perception of integrity varies from one situation to the next. Everyone has his own concept of right and wrong, but we all stray occasionally from our own standards. For example, if Leader A, who is regularly lauded for her good ethical judgment, occasionally makes personal copies on the organization's copy machine or uses the company's computer to surf the Internet on her lunch hour, is she being unethical? Although Leader A's sensibility informs her that these actions are inappropriate, she continues because she does not deem them harmful to the organization. This is an example of ethical relativism or contingency leadership. It provokes leaders into considering their own ethical anchors before facing complex situations.

> When you clarify the principles that will govern your life and the ends that you will seek, you give purpose to your daily decisions. A personal creed gives you a point of reference for navigating the sometimes stormy seas of organizational life. Without a set of such beliefs, your life has no rudder, and you are easily blown about by the winds of fashion. A credo to guide you prevents confusion on the journey.
>
> —James Kouzes and Barry Posner (2002)

THE CONCEPT IN PRACTICE

The ethical decisions of leaders, especially senior leaders, are observed more closely—and are likely to be more critiqued—than any other decisions the leaders make. These ethical dilemmas bear significant personal and professional risk because the resolutions to them often compel leaders to reveal their private opinions. How can leaders lessen this risk but still handle these ethical challenges? The following approaches serve as a guide.

Adopt an Organizational Code of Ethics

An organizational code of ethics defines appropriate and inappropriate conduct within the workplace and identifies conduct that falls between those poles. It protects the organization from legal entanglement and employees from harassment and unfair treatment. Leaders should be enlisted to support the code of ethics and should educate themselves and others about its application and benefits. Mechanisms to monitor employee adherence to the code must be developed as well.

The *Code of Ethics* and Ethical Policy Statement of the American College of Healthcare Executives, the leading professional association of healthcare leaders, is an excellent guide for practicing administrators, students, consultants, and others interested in the management field (see the *Code's* Preamble in Exhibit 5.1). Many healthcare organizations also have a corporate code of ethics or statement or corporate responsibility program. One example is presented in Exhibit 5.1.

Exhibit 5.1 Examples of Ethics Statements

Catholic Healthcare Partners Ethics Statement
Our ethical approach is embedded in how we care for patients, as well as in how we conduct our business relationships, treat our employees and respond to multiple stakeholders. While avoiding wrongdoing is a crucial consideration in such clinical and business decision-making, the principal focus of CHP's ethical discernment is to maximize the good that we are able to achieve on behalf of the people and communities we serve.

Preamble to ACHE's *Code of Ethics*
The purpose of the *Code of Ethics* of the American College of Healthcare Executives is to serve as a standard of conduct for affiliates. It contains standards of ethical behavior for healthcare executives in their professional relationships. These relationships include colleagues, patients or others served; members of the healthcare executive's organization and other organizations, the community, and society as a whole.

The *Code of Ethics* also incorporates standards of ethical behavior governing individual behavior, particularly when that conduct directly relates to the role and identity of the healthcare executive.

The fundamental objectives of the healthcare management profession are to maintain or enhance the overall quality of life, dignity and well-being of every individual needing healthcare service and to create a more equitable, accessible, effective and efficient healthcare system.

(continued)

(continued)

Healthcare executives have an obligation to act in ways that will merit the trust, confidence, and respect of healthcare professionals and the general public. Therefore, healthcare executives should lead lives that embody an exemplary system of values and ethics.

In fulfilling their commitments and obligations to patients or others served, healthcare executives function as moral advocates and models. Since every management decision affects the health and well-being of both individuals and communities, healthcare executives must carefully evaluate the possible outcomes of their decisions. In organizations that deliver healthcare services, they must work to safeguard and foster the rights, interests and prerogatives of patients or others served.

The role of moral advocate requires that healthcare executives take actions necessary to promote such rights, interests and prerogatives.

Being a model means that decisions and actions will reflect personal integrity and ethical leadership that others will seek to emulate.

Sources: Reprinted with permission from Catholic Healthcare Partners, Cincinnati, Ohio, and from ACHE, Chicago.

Some organizations create such statements to comply with regulatory requirements. However, a code of ethics should be established not only because it is the right thing to do but also because it is beneficial to the enterprise as a whole.

Adopt a Personal Code of Ethics

Writing a personal code of ethics, or credo, serves two purposes: (1) It resounds the values important to the person, and (2) it guides decision making and prioritizing when difficult issues come up. In adopting a credo, a leader should consider how other people perceive her behaviors and actions. As one CEO simply put it, "What do others think of you?"

Here are questions to ponder when developing a personal code of ethics:

- What does integrity mean to me?
- What do I value?
- What do I stand for?
- What am I willing to compromise or not compromise?

Committing to abide by this code of ethics is the next step. This commitment entails weighing the cost of not being ethical. The cost is significant, as illustrated by industry leaders who have been caught peddling dubious schemes, misappropriating funds, or behaving badly. Here are questions to consider in this regard:

- What damage will this situation cause my loved ones? My career and livelihood? My reputation in the community?
- Is the payoff worth everything I have worked hard to build?

Tell the Truth, and Do Not Exaggerate

> Hypocrisy, by its very nature, is self-invalidating. It is mind rejecting itself. A default on integrity undermines me and contaminates my sense of self. It damages me as no external rebuke or rejection can damage me.
>
> —Nathaniel Branden (1998)

In the strict ethical sense, telling the truth and not exaggerating are the same. Many people, however, differentiate the two. The argument for the difference is that telling the truth means telling no lies. On the other hand, exaggerating means stretching the truth to achieve a certain outcome or reaction.

For many, including healthcare executives, the latter has become accepted, commonplace practice. Many executives overestimate, engage in hyperbole, bend the facts, provide misquotes, twist the truth, and inappropriately expand their commentary to fit their needs. Whether discussing budget or organizational performance, many communications are filled with subjective stretches of the reality. Consider the following simple, but powerful, comments that are often rhetorical overstatements:

- "We have cut all the fat out of our budgets. All that remains is absolutely necessary."

- "I have told the team that many, many times. They must not be hearing me."
- "I don't think I can cut any deeper—it will hurt patient care."
- "Everyone is very upset about this."

How many times have you heard these or similar comments, and how many times have you fully believed them?

Do As You Say

Become known as a leader with follow-through. Often, integrity is measured less by failures in large significant areas and more by the lack of follow-up on little items. If a promise is made, it should be honored. One leader described it as having a high "say–do" ratio.

> Integrity implies clarity of values and/or direction, and behaviors consistent with them. While flexibility in thinking and approaches to challenges is an enormous asset for today's leaders, those who would follow their lead must be able to perceive in these leaders a core consistency in their fundamental values and actions.
>
> —Martin D. Merry (1996)

Use Power Appropriately

Effective leaders are acutely aware that power can be used for good or bad. They understand the sources of their power, and they use it judiciously. Unfortunately, ineffective leaders and some new executives wield their power to attempt to gain respect, prestige, and favors.

Admit Mistakes

Admitting mistakes is a noble, impressive act. However, too many leaders believe that such an admission weakens their authority. The opposite is true; power is not incrementally earned by perfection. Instead, power is what followers bestow on leaders. Followers can agree that admission of fault serves to increase their leader's power.

March to the Beat of Your Drum

A clear understanding of and commitment to personal values is a leader's greatest defense against the temptation of following a negative example. An executive who is guided first and foremost by her own ethical standards, not by popular opinion or practice, behaves and performs with integrity. This type of leader does not need to beat her drum loudly to gain followers; people will follow naturally.

Be Trustworthy

[Integrity is] accepting full responsibility, communicating clearly and openly, keeping promises, avoiding hidden agendas, and having the courage to lead yourself and your team or enterprise with honor, which includes knowing and being consistently honest with yourself, not only in mind but heart.

—Robert K. Cooper and Ayman Sawaf (1997)

In their book, *Judgment* Noel Tichy and Warren Bennis (2007, 84) state, "Leading with character gives the wise leader clear-cut advantages. They are easier to trust and follow; they honor commitments and promises; their word and behavior match; they are always engaged in and by the world; they are open to reflective 'backtalk'; they can admit errors and learn from their mistakes."

Author Stephen M. R. Covey (2008, 5) describes trust as the key way to avoid being viewed with suspicion; as such, trust reflects the essence of ethics and integrity. A leader is only as effective as the support that his followers grant him. Gaining that support is not possible if the leader does not earn others' trust and loyalty.

Manage Expense Accounts Judiciously

Leaders must require approvals for all reimbursements, especially for petty cash funds. This simple system of fund management does not create more bureaucracy, prevents temptation, and ensures that no one can question whether fund violation occurred.

Seasoned leaders agree that mismanagement of expenses is a common occurrence because it is so easy to overlook and undermine.

CONCLUSION

> Neither shall you allege the example of the many as an excuse for doing wrong.
>
> —**Exodus 23:2**

One of the greatest compliments to a leader is when others recognize her integrity and ethical uprightness. Ethics and integrity are always necessary ingredients in leadership. Leaders become great leaders when they follow their own moral instincts. It focuses them in times of uncertainty, strengthening their resolve to do right no matter what.

*   *   *

—————— **Self-Evaluation Questions** ——————

* What would others say about my integrity? About my ethics?
* Does integrity really mean that much to me? How many times have I not followed through? Not done what I said I would do? Not gotten back to someone when I promised I would?
* As the old saying goes, "Actions speak louder than words." How do I stack up against this saying?
* Do I appropriately use the power granted to me?
* Have I ever cut corners and behaved in an ethically questionable manner?

SUGGESTED READINGS

Bass, B., and P. Steidlmeier. 1999. "Ethics, Character, and Authentic Transformational Leadership Behavior." *Leadership Quarterly* 13: 169–91.

Knights, D., and M. O'Leary. 2006. "Leadership, Ethics and Responsibility to the Other." *Journal of Business Ethics* 67 (2): 125–37.

Maak, T. 2007. "Responsible Leadership, Stakeholder Engagement, and the Emergence of Social Capital." *Journal of Business Ethics* 74 (4): 329–43.

Manz, C. C., V. Anand, M. Joshi, and K. P. Manz. 2008. "Emerging Paradoxes in Executive Leadership: A Theoretical Interpretation of the Tensions Between Corruption and Virtuous Values." *Leadership Quarterly* 19 (3): 385–92.

Cases

Case 5.1

Jennifer Park, the chief financial officer of a hospital, is preparing for the year-end financial audit. She knows that several items in the books will draw the attention of the auditors. She meets with the CEO, Rob Cortez, to explain the situation. Rob responds with, "Make certain that there are no comments in the audit. The audit has to be clean because the chair is new, and he will not tolerate an audit adjustment. Do whatever it takes."

Questions

1. What is the implication of Rob's instruction to Jennifer?
2. What could happen behind the scenes if Jennifer follows Rob's order? If she does not follow his order?

Case 5.2

After checking references, Jerrod D'Amato, the human resources manager at a hospital, finds out that Cheryl Johnson, the number-one candidate for a critical care nursing position, was fired for absenteeism at her last job. Because the position has to be filled immediately and this discovery will only slow down the process, Jerrod chooses to withhold the information from the hiring nurse manager. He does discuss the issue with Cheryl, who tells him she was going through a tough time but is now ready for a new start. Jerrod thinks that Cheryl deserves a fair chance and her qualifications far outweigh the problems she had.

Questions

1. Is Jerrod right or wrong? Explain your reasoning.
2. Is there a difference between "need to know" information and "nice to know" information?

CHAPTER 6

Interpersonal Connection

Arthur Only had a reputation for being a great IT (information technology) manager at his hospital. He was always asked to serve on IT task forces and assigned to lead critical and difficult program implementations. Arthur, who has an MBA and a PhD in information technology, applied for the chief information officer (CIO) position when its incumbent retired. He got the job, beating other equally qualified but more experienced candidates. This promotion to CIO pleased many people at the hospital, but it was surprising given that Arthur was a middle manager, not necessarily next in line for the job. Among employees, the situation has become a favorite topic of discussion, including the following:

Employee A: How did Arthur do it, landing a big CIO job so fast? He never managed budgets and has never led a department. He never worked directly with senior management. Granted he was involved in many significant projects, but I can say the same for a lot of managers here, and they are not moving up the ladder.

Employee B: My cousin runs a large IT outsourcing firm. The turnover in these types of firms is very high. People frequently leave for more money, and worker loyalty is nonexistent. Somehow though, at my cousin's firm the turnover is low, although the employees could get so much more money if they worked somewhere else.

Employee A: Those people must be crazy!

Employee B: Maybe so, but my cousin is an ideal boss. He sets aside time during the day to visit his employees to listen to their concerns and input. He asks about their family, and he encourages them to take classes or go back to school so they can advance their careers. He respects their work, and he personally thanks them for their contributions. His employees feel welcomed in his office, and they know he puts people before numbers so they are not afraid to approach him. He is humble, supportive, and helpful. Doesn't my cousin sound like Arthur? Don't you think people would prefer to work for someone like him over someone whose main focus is always money and business?

> Leadership is a reciprocal relationship between those who choose to lead and those who decide to follow. Any discussion of leadership must attend to the dynamics of this relationship.
>
> —James Kouzes and Barry Posner (1993)

THE HEALTHCARE SYSTEM is the true industry of the people. No other industry witnesses human afflictions—from diseases of the body to ailments of the spirit; hosts the most basic human need—interaction at the most inopportune moments; and serves as the most common human thread—everyone needs healthcare. Because of these truths, people—patients, employees, physicians, volunteers, contractors, communities—are the critical factor in organizational success.

The irony is, although leading healthcare organizations find that improving relationships with their employees and patients is the key to excellence, most still focus on financial factors to measure their success. Every organization has an annual financial audit, but only a few conduct annual human resources audits, or even define what these human resources audits might be. Almost every board of trustees has a finance committee, but only a few have human resources committees. And most organizations have balanced scorecards, but the financial portion of these scorecards still receives the most time and attention.

In his well-known book *Good to Great*, Jim Collins (2001) writes about the "Level 5" leader: This person "builds enduring greatness through a paradoxical blend of personal humility and professional will." This type of leader puts people first (i.e., "get[s] the right people on the bus") and vision and strategy second. Financial success then follows this principle.

This chapter reiterates the significance of having people skills—a value so subtle that it can be easily undermined but so powerful that it can make or break an organization.

PEOPLE SKILLS

Leaders who have people skills are marked by a profound respect for the character of others and a deep faith in their potential, which is why they enjoy being with people and interact well with them. Often, the primary deciding factor in an executive search is the candidate's "chemistry" or ability to "blend" well with others, as illustrated in the vignette. Although almost all organizations place good people skills at the top of their recruitment-requirement list, they do not emphasize its importance to their existing employees and do not provide appropriate tools for measuring this attribute. Exhibit 6.1 lists the various definitions of "good people skills," as noted by other healthcare leaders.

The backbone of people skills is reciprocity, because without it no interaction or relationship occurs. Every healthy relationship—personal or professional—is marked by a mutual exchange, a quid pro quo of sorts. This exchange strengthens the bond and encourages its duration. Nonresponsive, uninvolved rank and file can discourage even the most interactive leader.

THE CONCEPT IN PRACTICE

The following are ways to enhance interpersonal connections.

Listen

Many leaders are leaders because they are the ones in the know. For example, subject-matter experts are designated to lead an initiative because of their knowledge and experience, not because of their ability to guide a group. Unfortunately, most of these leaders do too much talking, especially with subordinates, but not enough listening.

Hearing is easy because it is merely mechanical. Barring ear problems, we can all hear without exerting much effort. Listening, on the other hand, is a process that demands not only patience, time, energy, and respect but also an emotional and intellectual response. That is, listening is not (or should not be) a passive activity. In healthcare, many concerns are not articulated, if verbalized at all. Leaders must then listen more carefully to discover the root of a problem, and they must never assume the incorrect cliché "no news is good news."

Although listening is one of the most difficult tasks to master, especially in a high-stress, fast-paced environment, it is a critical skill. Exhibit 6.2 presents some techniques for improving listening.

Exhibit 6.1 Definitions of "Good People Skills"

- Practices active listening, and internalizes what others say so that she can reflect on it
- Is comfortable with his own humanity and readily admits mistakes and apologizes when necessary
- Is clear about her stance on an issue but respects others' perspectives
- Exhibits warmth, caring, and concern
- Has an air of genuineness and trustworthiness
- Gets along well with others
- Is open, is approachable, and cares about developing and sustaining strong relationships

---

Show Respect

In *Lions Don't Need to Roar,* author D. A. Benton (1992) suggests that "sincerity and positive regard are two things that just can't be faked, and you need both to deal with people effectively." When asked what bothers them most about senior management, many employees state that leaders do not appreciate what they do "in the trenches." Often, this means that executives do not make an effort to visit the units in which services are delivered; hence, they do not understand the stresses and challenges that frontline staff face on a regular basis. When leaders are absent, they cannot even thank, let alone become familiar with, those who do the work.

Strong leaders have great respect for others. They solicit their ideas, share pertinent information with them, encourage them to participate in organizational initiatives and activities, show regard

---

Exhibit 6.2 How to Enhance Listening Skills

Ask lots of questions. Often, the tone of your voice and the content of your questions can reveal your personal bias or opinion.

Ask clarifying questions. Do not assume the answers.

Restate the answers. Prevent misunderstanding by repeating or rephrasing in front of the person what he or she said.

Be open minded. People will tell you less if they feel you are judgmental.

Be receptive to bad news. Leaders who cannot take negative news are intimidating for the wrong reasons. "Don't kill the messenger" may be a cliché, but it is wise advice for every executive.

Minimize interruptions. Over-talking, acting distracted, taking phone calls, and answering e-mails are antithetical to good listening. Schedule a time for the discussion, and focus while it is happening.

Seek suggestions.

Involve others in the conversation. Ask those who are quiet for their thoughts; their perspectives often get lost in the discussion.

---

for their well-being, and recognize their hard work, among many other actions. As discussed in Chapter 4, "respect is the value that multiplies the desire of both the leader and follower to work harder and deliver consistently excellent performance."

Save Time for Staff

The workday of an average healthcare executive is hectic, leaving her little time for unscheduled interactions with her direct reports and other staff. As a result, she can be viewed as unapproachable, someone who is too important to mingle with the rank and file.

Scheduled employee events—staff meetings, picnics, organizational socials, award luncheons, retreats, holiday parties, and the like—are ideal for a busy executive to attend. These functions give the leader an opportunity to connect with many people, including staff, physicians, community members, and even patients and their families.

Manage Perceptions

Perception is more important than reality because people will believe what they imagine to be true, even if it is not the actual truth.

For example, the firing of a popular manager can set off a thousand impressions, most of which would be incorrect. Specifically, it could create irrational fears or breed gossip, both of which could harm the culture. In this scenario, ignoring the reaction is not an option. Giving the pat "It's a confidential issue" statement is not an option either.

What leaders could do, instead, is offer the most plausible explanation to minimize the perception that someone is hiding something. In this age of more transparent leadership, employees do not tolerate secrecy and lies. The more they perceive a cover-up or wrongdoing (true or not), the more they develop a distrust for their leaders.

Leaders also have to manage the various perceptions about their jobs. Expensive lunches, special parking spots, or any other privileges not enjoyed by the rest of the staff send the message that leaders are more valued by the organization. Although such perks do get offered in healthcare and other industries, they are not common. When leaders do receive (and accept) these perks, they must avoid the perception of any conflict of interest, something that they expect their employees to do.

> No matter how ambitious, capable, clear-thinking, competent...and witty you are, if you don't relate well to other people, you won't make it. No matter how professionally competent, financially adept, and physically solid you are, without an understanding of human nature, a genuine interest in the people around you, and the ability to establish personal bonds with them, you are severely limited in what you can achieve.
>
> —D. A. Benton (1992)

Recognize Others

Some leaders try to promote their own accomplishments by suggesting that they, rather than their direct reports, have done the good work. People-oriented leaders behave in the opposite manner—they highlight the skills and achievements of others, particularly their own staff members. They understand that leaders are measured by the successes of their teams or followers. Therefore, the more recognition the team members receive, the higher the leader is elevated and the greater the rewards to the team as a whole.

Manage and Channel Emotions Appropriately

Many leaders create problems for themselves by losing their temper and showing the negative side of their personality. Although everyone needs to vent, leaders must be careful not to lose control because uncontrolled emotions render them unprofessional, ineffective, helpless, and feared—qualities that impede genuine, equal interactions.

Moods—whether positive or negative—must be managed. Moodiness is usually seen as a symptom of poor mental health. If given a choice, most people would choose a constantly angry leader over a moody one because no guesswork is involved with the former.

Leaders who are in control of their emotions have good people skills. They remain calm in tense situations and focused in chaotic times. As a result, they are approachable by everyone else. Exhibit 6.3 presents tips on managing emotions.

Smile and Be Courteous

Many leaders would deem this suggestion silly; however, stories abound in executive search circles about executives who seem unapproachable because they are curt or do not smile. Zig Ziglar, a very

---

Exhibit 6.3 Simple Ways to Manage Emotions

Listen first, react second. By listening attentively to what is being said (e.g., suggestion, feedback, criticism, praise), you are delaying your natural impulse to react. True listening demands concentration, so it deflects attention and slows reaction time.

Change your mind-set and attitude. The workplace is not a battleground, regardless of the many "bullets" you must dodge in the course of the day. Therefore, do not prepare for any kind of battle, as doing so encourages negative and survivalist thinking.

Count to ten. If listening and having a positive attitude do not work, simply count to ten. This passing of time may dull the edges of your emotional response.

Cut off your anger as quickly as possible. Anger can be the biggest obstruction to reducing the charged nature of tense interpersonal situations.

(continued)

(continued)

Separate feelings from facts. Base discussions (or even arguments) on facts, not emotions or biases.

Be aware of your feelings' influence on your behavior. Realize that they can harm your judgment and abilities.

---

successful sales trainer and author, is well known for teaching and coaching executives about the power of a smile.

Visual, nonverbal cues communicate a leader's comfort with other people. For example, steady eye contact (without glaring or leering), smiling, and a relaxed posture send the message that a person is warm, caring, and friendly. These leaders create an atmosphere of trust and respect, where staff can state their opinions and not fear the repercussions.

Focus on the Needs of Followers

"Take care of them and they will take of you" is a phrase that echoes the most basic way for a leader to develop and maintain strong interpersonal connections with followers. Good executives do not take their staff's loyalty for granted, so they strive to get to know these individuals. They understand the significance of being fair, providing worthwhile work in a safe environment, and learning the things that matter most to people's professional and personal lives.

The recent upheavals in the healthcare industry—from chief executives committing fraud to the rise of medical errors and costs—have taken a toll on its workers and have caused the public to doubt its integrity. On top of this, workers have

> Despair means no choice, no options. Hope always provides options, always provides some glimmer of, "Yes, we can do it." That's what leaders have to communicate and embody and express in action.
>
> **—Warren Bennis and Robert Townsend (1997)**

endured large-scale downsizing and displacement, service cuts, and reorganization. At times like these, employees must feel and know that their leaders are representing their interest, and doing so well.

Show Compassion

A basic understanding of life's challenges and empathy for people's experiences underlie compassionate leadership. In the book *Strengths Based Leadership*, Tom Rath and Barry Conchie (2009, 163) write about effective leaders who lead with empathy: "Witnessing the happiness of others brings you pleasure. Consequently, you are likely to be attuned to opportunities to highlight people's success and positively reinforce their achievements. By doing do, you are likely to make a profound and engaging impression on that person." For example, many Catholic hospitals have maintained high employee morale and commitment. Those who have worked in these organizations will attest to the influence of the nuns in instilling compassion and concern for people.

Eliminate Childish, Unprofessional Behavior

Yelling, slamming doors, constantly complaining, gossiping, ignoring and then insulting others, bragging, and showing off are just some of the inappropriate behaviors that dishearten even the most patient peer or subordinate. Leaders who are secure with themselves and their position, status, and influence do not commit acts that disparage, belittle, or discredit others. Such behaviors breed intolerance, fear, low morale, poor productivity, secrecy, high turnover, and a dysfunctional culture.

Good leadership accommodates the needs and values of those who need to be led.

—Peter R. Scholtes (1998)

Be Optimistic

Optimism or hope, while difficult to define, can be a powerful motivator of good behavior. Leaders who have great interpersonal skills are eternal optimists. They inspire and encourage people to do their best. They rally projects that are languishing or behind schedule. They reinvigorate interest in smart but forgotten suggestions or decisions. They support innovation, action, and teamwork.

Dr. Stephen Mansfield, FACHE (2009), president and CEO of Methodist Health System in Dallas, opined,

> One of the most powerful emotions leaders can instill within their organization and among their organizational followers is hope. Hope, in an organizational context, is the dynamic intersection of optimism (individual and organizational willpower) and determination or persistence in the face of adversity (individual or organizational way-power). As a measurable construct, it has been demonstrated in the literature that higher hope organizations also have workforces that exhibit higher employee satisfaction and retention likelihood, as well as many other positive attributes, versus their lower hope organizational counterparts.

Being optimistic or hopeful can be learned, and sometimes it becomes an imperative for leaders during an especially difficult time, such as a financial downturn; reorganization because of a merger, an acquisition, or budget cuts; mass layoff; unionization; and staff shortage. Of course, optimism and hope are not enough to stem the tide of workplace change or fix the problem itself. However, it can do a lot to improve attitudes and mind-set.

Practice the Golden Rule

In the wildly popular book *All I Really Need to Know I Learned in Kindergarten,* author Robert Fulghum (1993) repeated simple lessons from childhood that resonated with people from all walks of life. Share everything. Play fair. Don't hit people. Put things back where you found them. Clean up your own mess. Don't take things that aren't yours. Say you are sorry when you hurt somebody. And so on.

The genesis of this book was Fulghum's experience with writing a personal credo (see Chapter 5 for a discussion on creating a personal code of ethics). In an increasingly cynical world, these "golden rules" may be deemed corny or unimaginative, but consider this: Healthcare fraud, including the highly reported white-collar crime by system chiefs, is almost always committed by those who have never understood the meaning of "do not take things that do not belong to you." The same can be said of hospital leaders who opted not to apologize to victims when their organizations caused harm or death as a result of a medical error, something that various studies indicate could have prevented a costly malpractice suit (see, for example, Berlin 2006). On the other hand, no leader who has "played fair" (i.e., was accountable, transparent) can be accused of wrongdoing.

CONCLUSION

Leadership is about building and maintaining relationships. The effectiveness of managing personal interactions is tied to how much leaders care about being with and working with others. Many years ago, the chair of a health administration graduate program warned me: "If you want to thrive in this business, you really have to love working with and around people. If you don't have a passion for that, go into another field." I cannot say it better.

———————— Self-Evaluation Questions ————————

* What does "people are our greatest asset" mean to me?
* Have I ever put other people down?
* Has anyone ever described me as a people person? Was this a source of pride for me?
* Has anyone ever described me as a good listener?

SUGGESTED READINGS

Carucci, R. 2006. "Building Relationships That Enable Next-Generation Leaders." *Leader to Leader* 42: 47–53.

Collins, J. 2001. *Good to Great: Why Some Companies Make the Leap... and Others Don't.* New York: HarperCollins.

———. 2001."Level 5 Leadership: The Triumph of Humility and Fierce Resolve." *Harvard Business Review* 79 (1): 66–79.

Duffy, F. D., G. H. Gordon, G. Whelan, and K. Cole-Kelly. 2004. "Assessing Competence in Communication and Interpersonal Skills: The Kalamazoo II Report." *Academic Medicine* 79 (6): 490–507.

Jouriles, N. J., C. L. Emerman, and R. K. Cydulka. 2002. "Direct Observation for Assessing Emergency Medicine Core Competencies: Interpersonal Skills." *Academy of Emergency Medicine* 9 (11): 1338–41.

McConnell, C. R. 2004. "Interpersonal Skills: What They Are, How to Improve Them, and How to Apply Them." *Health Care Management* 23 (2): 177–87.

Uhl-Bien, M. 2006. "Relational Leadership Theory: Exploring the Social Processes of Leadership and Organizing." *Leadership Quarterly* 17 (6): 654–76.

Cases

Case 6.1

James White has just finished a meeting with Teri Garr, his vice president, when he runs into Mary Briones, a peer departmental manager, in the hallway.

Mary: You're frowning. What's wrong?

James: Nothing. I'm fine.

Mary: You look stressed. You don't look like the regular enthusiastic James I know. Do you want to come into my office to talk about it?

James: Keep this between us, but Teri is impossible to read. Sometimes she is warm and approachable. Other times, she acts as if I'm a stranger. I just tried to discuss with her my desire to take on more responsibility, because I just earned a master's degree and I've worked here for four years. I wanted her advice on what I could do to get promoted.

Mary: Those are valid questions. What did she say?

James: She said, "You have too many projects right now. You shouldn't even be thinking of moving up." No explanation, no sugar coating. Then she said she had to go to another meeting. That's when I left.

Mary: No wonder you look dejected. Is there anything I can do to help?

Questions
1. How could Teri have handled the situation?
2. Is Mary displaying the interpersonal skills of a strong leader? How will these skills help James?

Case 6.2
Rosemary Brezinski, a veteran chief nursing officer, is the new president of a rapidly growing system hospital. Most of her impressive career has been spent in large tertiary organizations known for their research and medical innovations. Her new position is a significant promotion. She is now responsible for leading the hospital's response to the recent 10 percent growth in patient volume; improving morale and collaboration among managers, staff, and physicians; and planning and implementing the move of the system's teaching program to the hospital campus, something that only the senior management knows thus far.

In the first three weeks on the job, Rosemary has held several meetings with her senior management team and various leadership groups in the hospital. She has distributed to these leaders a detailed, 80-item list of priorities that will serve as the team's agenda for the next 18 months. She has informed them that she will assign each priority to an individual or a group. Her message to everyone has been consistent since the beginning of her tenure at the hospital: "I have never failed in the past. I expect that we will make these changes happen on time and on budget." In addition, she has not spoken to the medical staff or the frontline employees.

Questions

1. What interpersonal connection mistakes has Rosemary committed so far?
2. How do you think the staff (including the physicians and managers) feel about her style?
3. Will her mandates for change work?

CHAPTER 7

Servant Leadership

"What is your primary role as a leader?" Sister Mary O'Hara, the president and chief executive officer of a soon-to-open community hospital, asked her newly formed management team. The answers varied:

- Work toward our mission and vision
- Get everyone to work cooperatively
- Manage efficiently and effectively
- Meet our goals and make sure our employees do their jobs

Sister Mary responded, "All of these are good ideas. What I want you to keep in mind most of all is this: Each of you is a servant leader. By that I mean that your job is to serve those who report to you. Help them do their work, and let them help you do yours. Be humble. You do not know all the answers and you are not the experts, so seek out input from others. Give credit and praise liberally, and be generous with your time regardless of how busy you become. Listen before you speak. Ask how you can lend a hand. Teach and encourage learning. I realize that some of you may have a different view of leadership than what I just laid out. But the mission of our community hospital is to serve, and that is exactly what we are going to do— we will serve each other, regardless of our titles."

The management team applauded loudly in agreement.

THE HEALTHCARE INDUSTRY was established with a simple, altruistic purpose: to serve the public. Therefore, its leaders must subscribe to the same edict by becoming "servants" to the needs of their organizations and constituents. Servant leadership is not merely a trendy practice borne by political correctness or a clichéd intonation of "following to lead"; instead, it is a management style that delivers desired outcomes, boosts morale, strengthens the organizational structure, and yields support for the leader.

Robert Greenleaf (2009), the father of servant leadership, defined the concept this way:

> The servant-leader is servant first…. It begins with the natural feeling that one wants to serve, to serve *first*. Then conscious choice brings one to aspire to lead. That person is sharply different from one who is *leader* first, perhaps because of the need to assuage an unusual power drive or to acquire material possessions…. The leader-first and the servant-first are two extreme types. Between them there are shadings and blends that are part of the infinite variety of human nature.

A servant leader is marked by the following characteristics:

1. Focuses on the needs of followers
2. Eschews selfish behavior, personal biases, and pursuit of personal ambition
3. Sincerely respects all people
4. Realizes that the contributions of followers are what enable the organization to fulfill its mission
5. Helps, encourages, and counsels followers to hone their skills and become better at their positions because doing so brings the organization closer to its goals

Since it was first theorized in the 1970s, servant leadership has gained a great following, including experts in management and organizational behavior such as Peter Senge, Stephen Covey, Margaret Wheatley, and Ken Blanchard. Exhibit 7.1 contrasts traditional leadership from servant leadership.

Servant leaders give their skills, time, talent, knowledge, and other capabilities to improve their organizations and, by extension, the lives of their staff and service communities. They listen intently to the needs,

Exhibit 7.1 Difference Between Traditional Leadership and Servant Leadership

Traditional leadership	Servant leadership
Motivation: To lead	Motivation: To serve
Approach: Top-down, command and control	Approach: Bottom-up, collaborative
Basis: Power and authority	Basis: Stewardship
Primary focus: Finance	Primary focus: People
Self-awareness not important	Self-awareness critical
Followers may/may not grow	Followers definitely grow

wants, and opinions of those they serve through informal conversations, surveys, focus groups, and market studies (*BizTimes* 2009).

Also, servant leaders are role models and teachers. They set an example for others, as one CEO has done: "I gave each executive in the organization a small rock and a small ceramic monkey to place on their desks. The purpose of the rock and the monkey is to help them to be always mindful of what they need to do—keep the rocks and barriers out of the way so their staff can do their jobs. And if the staff can do their jobs, they won't put inappropriate monkeys on their back." Another CEO echoes this principle: "My job is to take away any obstacles that keep [my direct reports] from succeeding.... If there's an obstacle between you and any of our targets, I need to know about it."

Essentially, servant leaders' success depends on how well they meet their followers' needs. Followers are more efficient, productive, and satisfied when given autonomy, support, resources, and positive examples. As a result, they perform better than expected and grow personally and professionally. More important, they are more likely to become servants themselves.

Servant leadership may be likened to *transformational leadership* in that both philosophies "show concern for their followers, [but] the overriding focus of the servant leader is upon service to their followers. The transformational leader has a greater concern for getting followers to engage in and support organizational objectives" (Williams and Jones 2009).

THE CONCEPT IN PRACTICE

The following guidelines can hone a leader's servant skills.

Share Information

> A new moral principle is emerging which holds that the only authority deserving one's allegiance is that which is freely and knowingly granted by the led to the leader in response to, and in proportion to, the clearly evident servant stature of the leader.
>
> —Robert K. Greenleaf (1983)

Sharing information, not on a need-to-know basis, with peers and subordinates opens communication pathways through which ideas travel. An open exchange of ideas signifies the leader's respect for other perspectives and trust in others' ability to contribute. Although information is power, a servant leader is disinclined to abuse the knowledge he acquired to manipulate the situation for his own good.

Delegate Authority

Delegation not only increases productivity but also promotes teamwork, especially during times of crisis (although many leaders tend to take the reins when serious problems arise). In a crisis situation, servant leaders are not apprehensive about delegating authority to their direct reports because they have regularly included and coached them in brainstorming, problem solving, decision making, and implementation. Thus, these leaders are confident of their staff's ability to perform under great stress.

Delegating authority should be a frequent practice in healthcare organizations because the challenges and responsibilities are often too intricate for one person to handle alone. In addition, frontline staff directly face the everyday dilemmas in the workplace and therefore often have more practical and sustainable solutions than supervisors, directors, and vice presidents can offer. Servant leaders are aware of this dynamic.

The greater the degree to which the vision is shared by employees and addresses their deepest aspirations, the greater the likelihood the leader will be seen as charismatic.

—Jay Conger (1989)

Live the Mission and Pursue the Vision

Most mission statements of healthcare organizations include the word "serve." Servant leaders take their missions to heart. They ensure that the organizational vision, values, culture, strategies, and activities are consistent with the mission. They enlist others, including physicians, in establishing policies and practices that support and advance the mission.

Servant leaders are also visionaries. They are future-oriented and innovative, so they seek to understand past events and current realities—any factors that have an impact on the future operation of the organization. They look to staff to participate in this visioning work, aware that such an engagement facilitates the achievement of the vision.

Support and Promote Continuing Education

All employees can pursue continuing education to enhance their professional or vocational skills, which consequently improves their job marketability. Servant leaders not only apportion organizational funds to finance staff's educational pursuits (e.g., degree programs, professional seminars, certification courses) but also provide coaching.

"Teaching moments"—occasions that leaders can take to explain an organizational decision, policy, process, practice, or stance—are an excellent way to both inform and engage the staff. For example, an adverse medical event is a teaching moment, wherein leaders can review the safety standards, reiterate the quality policy, delineate the role of staff, and exchange questions and ideas about improvement.

Most important, professional and personal development must go beyond lip service. Policies (and budget) that support continuing education must be in place. Specifically, performance expectations should include a requirement to complete a certain number of continuing education hours by the next performance review. The onus of checking up on this requirement must fall on the leader.

Provide Opportunities for Accomplishments

Servant leaders do not set up their followers to fail. Structured objectives and clear instructions help staff reach their goals and complete their assignments. Servant leaders provide coaching and support when needed, but they allow staff freedom to work toward their objectives. In doing so, staff gain mastery of their jobs, greater enjoyment from their work, confidence, new skills, and feelings of achievement. They are proud to say "we did this ourselves."

Establish a Succession Plan

The sudden departure of a leader (voluntarily or involuntarily) can cause much chaos and uncertainty within the organization. Worse is when no succession plan is in place that details that leader's replacement. The oldest baby boomers are expected to retire in the next five years, although the current recession may decelerate this trend. Regardless of this trend, succession planning must be a priority for all leaders, especially those who are nearing retirement.

Although healthcare executives are cognizant of the importance of succession planning, they do not engage in the practice readily. According to one study that yielded 722 responses, "the most frequently cited reason for not conducting succession planning: It is not a high enough priority right now (46 percent). Other reasons cited were because the current CEO is too new (31 percent) and there is no internal candidate to prepare (25 percent)" (Garman and Tyler 2007). Conversely, succession planning is a priority for servant leaders because their first priority is the needs of their employees, which include strong and dependable leadership.

Learn About the Work

When employees complain that their leaders are "out of touch," they are mostly right. Leaders cannot empathize with frontline staff if they do not understand what their work entails. Visiting the units and talking with staff are some strategies for learning the work. But leaders could go a step further by shadowing employees and interacting with patients and their families.

Servant leaders partake in these experiences, enabling them to encounter firsthand the difficulties they only hear about, to speak the language of caregivers and support staff, and to discover areas for improvement. In the process, servant leaders and the staff get to know each other better, paving the way for mutual understanding of their distinct roles.

> Being a servant may not be what many leaders had in mind when they chose to take responsibility for the vision and direction of their organization or team, but serving others is the most glorious and rewarding of all leadership tasks.
>
> —James Kouzes and Barry Posner (1993)

Mentor Others

Clearly, healthcare executives are pressed for time, and mentoring often becomes a casualty in all this. Mentoring is a critical competency that sets apart good leaders from great ones (see Dye and Garman 2006). Servant leaders are advocates for personal and professional development. As such, they provide coaching and support continuing education.

Hold Simple Celebrations

Servant leaders are acutely aware of the morale-boosting capability of simple celebrations and praise. A round of applause during a staff meeting, an acknowledgment in an organization-wide publication or the intranet, or a plate of cookies is a small gesture that carries great weight. For example, one chief financial officer held a pizza party for the credit and collection staff when they met their monthly numbers. The employees were touched and motivated to repeat their achievement.

Change the Focus of Performance Reviews

Annual or mid-year performance reviews are often met with dread. The main reason for this mind-set is that the focus of these assessments is criticism—what mistakes were committed, what goals were not accomplished, what skills were not improved. As a result, the feedback is taken as a personal offense, not as a constructive comment. No one wants to feel attacked, so no one enjoys this type of review.

Servant leaders are aware of this reaction, so they structure the performance evaluation differently:

- The focus is future performance, not past missteps or lost opportunities.
- Achievement of objectives is celebrated. Goals were developed with input from the employee and with consideration of the person's ability, environmental obstacles, available resources, and realistic timelines. Then, they were monitored during the year.
- No blame is placed, and the factors that contributed to instances of poor performance are discussed so that they are corrected or eliminated.
- Ongoing development is encouraged, regardless of how high the rank of the employee.

Make a Connection with Staff

Servant leaders are not aloof or detached. They maintain relationships and stay abreast of issues that affect all of their associates—staff, physicians, board members, community leaders, and peers.

Making a connection could be as simple as visiting departments or attending organizational events or as involved as getting to know the staff. Perhaps one of the best ways a leader can make a connection is by showing employees that she is one of them, as this example from Andrea Price, FACHE (2009), chief operations officer of Mercy Health Partners, illustrates:

> Servant-leadership is providing a framework from which many thousands of known and unknown individuals are helping to improve how we treat those who do the work within our many institutions. Servant-leadership truly offers hope and guidance for a new era in human development, and for the creation of better, more caring institutions.
>
> —**Larry Spears (2004)**

I lead by putting people first, whether or not they report to me. It's my duty to help other people succeed, so I provide as much support, coaching, encouragement, feedback, and guidance as necessary. I also give them a chance to demonstrate their skills and knowledge so that they can become aware of their own strengths and weaknesses. I serve as a resource to my staff, readily available to address their needs.... There is nothing that goes on in the hospital that I am unwilling to do, regardless of my title. I have mopped spills off the floor in my suit and heels, much to the amazement of the staff. While I was rounding late one night, I met a patient who was hungry for a salad. I went to the cafeteria and prepared a salad according to how the patient wanted it. As a healthcare executive, I can't give medication, but I can get water for a patient.

CONCLUSION

Picture an organization in which everybody performs every activity with the primary intention of serving someone else. It seems like utopia, but it is achievable, and it starts with leaders. If subordinates feel that their leaders serve them, they will likely model that behavior toward others. As a result, service to patients will be enhanced, improving the organization's competitive advantage.

✳ ✳ ✳

——————————— **Self-Evaluation Questions** ———————————

* Why am I in the leadership position?
* What is my leadership style? Does it place a heavy emphasis on controlling others?
* Does the idea of serving others make me think that I am a weak leader?

SUGGESTED READINGS

Garber, J. S., E. A. Madigan, E. R. Click, and J. J. Fitzpatrick. 2009. "Attitudes Towards Collaboration and Servant Leadership Among Nurses, Physicians and Residents." *Journal of Interprofessional Care* 23 (4): 331–40.

Greenleaf.org. This website includes an extensive list of resources and publications.

Joseph, E. E., and B. E. Winston. 2005. "A Correlation of Servant Leadership, Leader Trust, and Organizational Trust." *Leadership and Organization Development Journal* 26 (1): 6–22.

Neill, M. W., and N. S. Saunders. 2008. "Servant Leadership: Enhancing Quality of Care and Staff Satisfaction." *Journal of Nursing Administration* 38 (9): 395–400.

Neubert, M. J., K. M. Kacmar, D. S. Carlson, L. B. Chonko, and J. A. Roberts. 2008. "Regulatory Focus as a Mediator of the Influence of Initiating Structure and Servant Leadership on Employee Behavior." *Journal of Applied Psychology* 93 (6): 1220–33.

Stone, A. G., R. F. Russell, and K. Patterson. 2004. "Transformational Versus Servant Leadership: A Difference in Leader Focus." *Leadership and Organization Development Journal* 25 (4): 349–61.

Sturm, B. A. 2009. "Principles of Servant-Leadership in Community Health Nursing." *Home Health Care Management & Practice* 21 (2): 82–89.

Case and Exercise

Case 7.1

Two students in an executive seminar, Rachel Goh and Jared Kaufman, explore the basis of servant leadership in class:

Rachel: I don't buy it. The idea that servant leaders are more committed to their followers and organization sounds too religious for me. The fact is, people are, at the core, selfish. We act with self-interest, first and always.

Jared: Servant leaders are manipulative, but in a good way. Take me, for example. My staff cannot get along well without me because I provide them with everything they need, from advice to tangible resources. This is a win-win situation. I support their work, and in exchange I get the results I want.

Questions

1. Do you agree with this summation that servant leadership is (a) not possible given the selfish nature of people and (b) secretly or outwardly manipulative but harmless? Explain your answer.
2. Using Robert Greenleaf's definition of this theory (see www.greenleaf.org), discuss how servant leadership can guide executives in today's healthcare environment.

Exercise 7.1

Servant leadership is likely to work best in an organizational culture that supports it. That is, some cultures have a high level of trust and team orientation, while others are hierarchical or rely on command-and-control principles.

Question

1. What types of culture can support the practice of servant leadership?

See the following websites for a discussion on organizational culture:
- http://managementhelp.org/org_thry/culture/culture.htm
- www.soi.org/reading/change/culture.shtml

- www.au.af.mil/au/awc/awcgate/ndu/strat-ldr-dm/pt4ch16.html
- www.tnellen.com/ted/tc/schein.html
- http://cims.ncsu.edu/downloads/Research/71_WDWK_culture.pdf

CHAPTER 8

Desire to Make a Change

Several years ago, Elaine Rostovich asked her boss Barb Valdez why she gave up overtime pay and shift differentials to become a nurse manager. Barb answered, "The loss in pay does not matter to me as much as the frustration of not being able to make improvements around here. As a staff nurse, I couldn't change anything that was no longer working. Sure I do a lot more paperwork and face more stress now, but it is satisfying to see that our clinical outcomes are better and our staff and patients are happier because we are now more efficient."

Barb's reasoning finally makes sense to Elaine as she listens to her mentor emphasize the importance of leading change: "Like many healthcare CEOs, I entered the field because I wanted to make a difference in people's lives. This topic has not been researched a lot, but that desire is the true beginning of improvement. Those who have this passion work hard to make positive changes happen, and they don't do it for money, praise, or prestige. They do it because they understand that nothing is beyond improvement. And they use all their resources, skills, and knowledge to accomplish their goals. They are some of the most well-informed people around, these change leaders."

THE DESIRE TO make a change is one of the most distinctive values of a strong leader. *Change makers,* as these leaders are known, are high achievers. They actively seek out flaws in the system and implement improvements. While scouts abide by the rule "leave a campsite in better condition than you found it," change makers initiate upgrades even before they get to the campsite. They are proactive, are innovative, and welcome challenges.

CHARACTERISTICS OF A CHANGE MAKER

Our current success is the best reason to change things.

—Iwao Isomura (1998)

In the 1960s, motivational theorist David McClelland posited that individuals who have achievement motivation, as is the case with change makers, are likely to be goal-oriented and uphold high standards of performance. These individuals are most likely to move into leadership positions because they can operate well and even flourish despite the high levels of stress and unceasing demands for long hours, critical thinking, and quick turnarounds.

Change makers have *restless discontent*—the inability to live with the status quo. They cannot tolerate ineffective processes that force people to muddle through ill-conceived standards and processes. One CEO defined this discontent as an "ability to sense opportunities." It is a fitting description, as change makers are constantly on the lookout for new ideas. The discontent peels away as areas for improvement garner attention and the need for change earns buy-in from others, especially senior management.

For many leaders, the desire to make a change becomes a professional calling. This is evident in the quality improvement movement in healthcare, which calls on the industry to

- establish measurable goals and standards,
- develop systems for monitoring progress toward and achieving desired outcomes,
- disseminate lessons learned,
- celebrate successes, and
- continue the improvement efforts.

THE CONCEPT IN PRACTICE

Pay Equal Attention to All Measures of Performance

In flight school, pilots are taught how to maneuver their planes with the guidance of merely their instrument panel. This technique teaches pilots how to fly safely despite the hindrances that may surround them—thick fog, utter darkness, raging storms, or other conditions that impair visibility. However, some pilots tend to pay the most attention to the altimeter, which tells the position and location of the plane on the horizon. Although the altimeter is an important gauge, it is not the only instrument a pilot should rely on. Trouble almost always ensues when the other critical measures are overlooked. This is also true in healthcare management.

Change Makers Have Achievement Motivation

In his classic text, David McClelland (1961) posited the following attributes of people with achievement motivation:

1. High achievers address problems rather than leave them to chance.
2. The goals of high achievers can be accomplished; they are neither too difficult nor too easy.
3. High achievers are more interested in accomplishment than in rewards.
4. High achievers seek workplaces and positions that offer ample feedback.
5. High achievers constantly think about improvement, excellence, and perfection. They seek out organizations that will allow them to make changes.

All healthcare leaders—new or seasoned—have, at one point or another, focused only on the financial report when determining the status of their organization. This is an understandable practice; after all, without funds the operation will cease to exist, an especially salient issue in an environment filled with bankruptcies and acquisitions. However, healthcare is hardly a one-dimensional enterprise. If too much priority is given to revenue, capital, debt, investment, and other elements of finance, then not enough attention is given to human resources, patient safety, clinical outcomes, quality improvement, physician relations, and the like.

Change makers understand that the organization is a system and thus needs a system-based approach. Simply, a flaw in one component can cause damage to another, ushering in a cascading effect.

Turn Satisfied Employees Into Engaged Employees

High-performing organizations tend to have highly satisfied workers. However, satisfaction does not lead to engagement. Many happy employees walk in and out of their jobs daily without a desire to participate in the activities that cause their happiness. Or they may ignore areas that could use improvement because they think bringing about change is not part of their job responsibilities.

Gallup (2009b) polls in the past decade, which involved more than 1.2 million healthcare workers, revealed that engaged employees

- "are more productive;
- are more focused on their patients' care and treatment;
- are safer, stay with their employers longer, and set a positive example of engagement for others throughout the organization; and
- are more profitable for a provider than disengaged employees."

Note that more and more human resources firms are conducting employee engagement (as opposed to "satisfaction") surveys today. This signals a shift in mind-set: Good employees have much to contribute to the viability of the organization. Seeking participation from employees could also bring out the latent change makers among them. Jim Haudan (2009), the CEO of Root Learning, emphasizes that for change and improvement to be fully executed, employees at all levels must be given the opportunity to internalize the thinking and rationale behind the strategy. Haudan reiterates that the most effective leaders create environments where employees are highly engaged.

Be Objective Driven and Progress Oriented

Change makers are passionate about setting objectives for both professional and organizational purposes. Doing so helps them measure the effectiveness of their and others' performance, decisions, and activities. Many leaders fail to set clear goals, delaying or impeding progress and achievement and frustrating those involved.

In addition, change makers admit that even the best organizations (and employees) must evolve with the times. Thus, they push to move forward, tracking their steps along the way with available measurement tools. S.M.A.R.T.—Specific, Measurable, Attainable, Realistic, and Timely—is still the best strategy for setting goals, although it is now more than a decade old (see Kouzes and Posner 1993 for more information). S.M.A.R.T. goals allow organizations to focus simultaneously on the present and the future.

> An effective vision integrates into the organization's purpose and into the employee's job a sense of contribution to themselves, to an industry, or to society. This sense of worthiness and influence can lead to greater commitment, enthusiasm, and the motivation to work harder.
>
> —Jay A. Conger (1989)

Welcome Change

Change makers enjoy new challenges and are not afraid of taking risks. For them, change is a normal part of leadership and presents opportunities. As such, they prefer to err on the side of overstudying or overanalyzing trends than to be misinformed. Being prepared serves as a weapon against the unknown or sudden change that seems unmanageable.

The fear of making the wrong decision is endemic in healthcare. On the clinical side, an error could result in injury or death and subsequently costly and drawn-out lawsuits. On the business side, an error could result in loss of customers and consequently revenue. Certainly, cautious decisions are in order.

However, this does not mean risks should not be taken. Progress and innovation—two words that most leaders would like to be associated with—are not driven by fear. They are possible only with leaps, albeit calculated, of faith.

Celebrate Accomplishments

As discussed in Chapter 7, people enjoy celebrations, especially if they highlight the product of their hard work. A celebration of accomplishments not only embodies the joy, relief, and pride of the team, it also resounds the gratitude of the leaders. People who are able to see that their efforts have made a difference and are appreciated are likely to repeat their performance in the future and feel empowered. Empowerment is a strong motivation because it makes people feel in control and valued.

Celebrations may also be used to improve morale. For example, one executive organized a monthly "Breakfast of Champions" for employees. Individuals and departments who made progress toward goals were recognized during the program and given a box of Wheaties cereal as a token of appreciation.

Establish a Problem-Solving Method

Change makers follow specific approaches, such as the following, to solving a problem:

- Identify the problem and describe it explicitly, including the effects it has on staff, operations, the bottom line, current and future goals, and patients.
- Perform a root-cause analysis.
- Generate (or brainstorm) solutions, and weigh the pros and cons of each option.
- Select the best solution.
- Develop clear objectives with measures, including timelines and standards.
- Assign clear roles and responsibilities to those involved in the task.
- Implement the solution.
- Monitor progress, making corrections or adjustments along the way if necessary.

- Communicate with all stakeholders throughout the process.
- Evaluate the process afterward.

Continue to monitor the cause of the problem to ensure no recurrence takes place.

Learn Contemporary Quality Improvement Concepts

Lean management and Six Sigma are just some of the many tools that leaders can use to improve processes and manage change. Some instruments, such as those developed by the Institute for Healthcare Improvement, are specific to healthcare, but many are adopted from other industries. Change makers stay current about modern improvement techniques, aware of their advantages, disadvantages, and applications.

Be Willing to Do More

By nature, change makers are always looking for areas to refine, enhance, or study. For some leaders, this could mean increasing the number of their accomplishments for the organization, participating in task forces or forming new ones, or volunteering for new assignments. For others, this could mean expanding their control or creating a new service line. Those who seek added responsibilities or aim for higher achievements may be accused of feeding the needs of their ego. However, the results of this willingness to do more are often beneficial to the organization. They yield enhancements not previously thought of.

Network and Benchmark

Change makers are competitive, compelled to compare their results and practices with those of others. They are drawn to data and measurement tools, and they keep abreast of current approaches to forecast future standards. As such, they interact frequently with peers and insiders, visit other sites to scope out new technology and initiatives, and attend conferences and workshops. Simply, these leaders take advantage of any networking opportunity to stay informed, competitive, and innovative.

In contrast, leaders who seldom network and benchmark lose their creative spark and even their perspective. Their strategies and decision making are informed by outdated assumptions.

Learn Change Management

Today one of the most requested attributes of a leader is the ability to manage and bring about change. Change management is a structured process that uses various leadership theories and management models. Although not new, the concept has garnered renewed interest in these times of constant change. Change expert John Kotter (1996, 2002) enumerates the basic components of change management:

Step 1: Create urgency
Step 2: Form a powerful coalition
Step 3: Create a vision for change
Step 4: Communicate the vision
Step 5: Remove obstacles
Step 6: Create short-term wins
Step 7: Build on the change
Step 8: Anchor the change in the corporate culture

Make a Change for Progress's Sake, Not Yours

Some leaders get involved in change efforts because of an inappropriate and selfish need to gain personal fame. They take credit for other people's work and bask in the glory of accomplishment, but they contribute little and pass on the blame if something goes wrong. This is not the behavior of change makers.

Change makers pursue change and improvement for the sake of progress, not to strengthen their power or build up admirers and followers who shower them with adulation and gifts.

> Maintaining an unrelenting focus on people, performance, and change, however, demands courage. When the mechanistic organization gives way to the profoundly human challenge of broad-based, behavior-driven change, managers can no longer rely on traditional sources of authority or the power of decisions.
>
> —**Douglas K. Smith (1996)**

CONCLUSION

The leader's value of wanting to make a change is admirable, as it benefits the individual, the organization, and everyone else in between. Change makers strengthen the organization's competitive advantage and reputation, and they help keep out mediocre and stagnant practices and strategies.

✳ ✳ ✳

—————— Self-Evaluation Questions ——————

* What have I accomplished that could be my hallmark of service?
* If I were to leave my organization today, how would I be missed? Have I left a "mark" in the organizations in which I've worked?
* Flood lines along riverbanks indicate the height the water reached. If I used this parallel to measure my achievement, how high is my flood line?

SUGGESTED READINGS

Cangemi, J. P., B. Burga, H. Lazarus, R. L. Miller, and J. Fitzgerald. 2008. "The Real Work of the Leader: A Focus on the Human Side of the Equation." *Journal of Management Development* 27 (10): 1026–36.

Carnevale, D. G. 2001. "Leadership, Innovation, and Organizational Change in Public Organizations." *American Review of Public Administration* 31 (18): 218–30.

Case and Exercise

Case 8.1

Kristen Photakis, CEO of a rural hospital, is talking with her friend Jason Weiss, a long-term healthcare consultant about ways to better engage senior and departmental managers.

Kristen: It's frustrating that they sit back and wait for me to create the agenda, give them assignments, or study new trends.

Jason: How does the hospital develop strategies?

Kristen: We hold an annual board retreat. During that time, the board and I come up with 25 to 30 goals. When I return to the office, I meet with the vice presidents [VPs] to tell them what was discussed. Then I draft subgoals for each of the major objectives identified at the board retreat. The VPs and I hammer out the details until we come up with specific strategies and work plans.

Jason: There are three things wrong with that process. First, everything is developed at the top of the organization with little or no input from the lower ranks. Second, you have gotten into the habit of creating everyone's work plans rather than giving people the chance to develop their own. Third, you and the board set too many goals. You have to consider current workload and priorities, previous commitments, unfinished strategies, et cetera. No one can possibly keep up with all the details.

Kristen: Sounds like I have work to do.

Jason: Keep in mind that change is a group effort, not a solo practice. If you want your staff to get involved, you have to get out of the way and let them in.

Questions

1. Is the consultant correct? Explain your answer.
2. What can Kristen do to improve the situation she has created?

Exercise 8.1

The Institute for Healthcare Improvement (IHI, see www.ihi.org) has had a profound impact on change and quality improvement in healthcare. Among IHI's many innovations is rapid-cycle testing, an approach to trying out an idea on a small scale before it is widely implemented. During the testing, the idea is modified if needed and then tried again; the cycle continues until the ideal result is achieved. In the end, the idea is made permanent and is applied on a larger scale. A key component of rapid-cycle testing is the collection of small sets of data that can be quickly analyzed. These data samples must be carefully picked to ensure that they are representative of the larger data set.

Questions

1. How can rapid-cycle testing improve or harm a leader's ability to make a change?
2. Name other improvement strategies used in the industry today.

CHAPTER 9

Commitment

Judith D'Amato and Bob Graham, both seasoned vice presidents at a large medical center, are talking about Blake Cullen, the newly appointed chief executive officer.

Judith: I am amazed at how different she is from the last two CEOs—Larry Orestes specifically.

Bob: Exactly! Larry practically lived here. He worked more hours than anyone did and rarely took a vacation. To his credit, he accomplished a lot. But I can't tell you of a single project that was not contentious or that followed the initial agreed-on plan. He hated delegating or having others take the lead. He was exhausting. That's probably why he's not here anymore.

Judith: Blake's energy and focus are admirable. She has a thick file for every initiative we have rolled out. She asks questions and pores over material. Despite her packed schedule, she seems to have the time to attend staff events and she welcomes people in her office. She's pleasant to be around, and she doesn't intimidate anyone with her skills and high rank.

Bob: Plus, she's so secure with her role that she's not threatened when someone else has better ideas. In fact, she invites and expects us to be part of the process, to do our job. The one thing she strongly demands is that we always keep the mission and vision at the forefront of all our activities.

Judith: It's also clear that she has a life outside of the hospital. Did you know she runs marathons with her grown kids? And every summer, she and her family spend two weeks volunteering to rebuild homes and plant trees in a depressed urban area. One of my nurses told me that. I was inspired.

Bob: That may be one of the major differences between Blake and Larry. She's here because she loves the job and respects the work we do. He was here because he was padding his resume for the next big move.

EFFECTIVE LEADERSHIP IS a demanding master. It yields not to time. It bends not to excuses. It accepts only commitment.

Commitment is a value that measures the leader's dedication to his profession. Because commitment binds the executive to his work, it generates a strong work ethic, loyalty, pride, productivity, ownership, and even joy.

In Exhibit 9.1, several healthcare executives offer their own definition of commitment. Some of these definitions use a sports analogy, equating the leader to an athlete and commitment to her drive and competitiveness. The primary reason for this is that many leaders view their roles and responsibilities as an athletic event for which they continually train physically, mentally, emotionally, and spiritually.

Great leaders simultaneously act as coaches and players, inspiring and guiding others to do well and performing the work themselves. These leaders are also cheerleaders, boosting morale and applauding efforts. Some of the more popular motivational speakers at leadership conferences are sports coaches, such as Lou Holtz and Joe Paterno, as well as athletes who have overcome personal difficulties, such as Lance Armstrong.

Exhibit 9.1 Commitment as Defined by Healthcare Executives

- "Getting the job done. You face all the hurdles and finish the race."

- "An attitude of excitement about any problem. Being committed means that you have the chance to fix it."

- "Having a solemn covenant that you will do whatever it takes to fulfill the mission of your organization."

- "The old story of the chicken and the pig. The chicken gave eggs but the pig gave his life. That is true commitment. In some ways, I feel as though I have done the same for the healthcare organizations I have worked for."

- "Giving your all because any race worth running is a race worth winning."

THE CONCEPT IN PRACTICE

Commitment to the profession is not a given in healthcare, especially in the current environment of high demands but low returns. The following simple strategies help in maintaining commitment.

Stay Focused on the Vision

The organizational vision can serve as a lighthouse and a compass for stewards navigating the choppy waters of healthcare management. It illuminates and points to the path to take. The vision, assuming it was not established arbitrarily and was the result of a careful participative process, takes away the guesswork and indecision about the future state of the organization. Commitment to the cause, so to speak, is easier with this desired outcome in full view. Great leaders prefer to know where they are going before they even start the journey.

Weigh Work and Life Pursuits

The ultimate test of a servant leader's work is whether those served develop toward being more responsible, caring, and competent individuals.

—Richard Hughes, Robert Ginnett, and Gordon Curphy (2009)

In recent years, the option to work from home has become a sought-after benefit for many workers. Many leaders and managers, however, have been exercising this capability for as long as reports and deadlines have been around. The availability of wireless technology has exacerbated this practice, equipping leaders to work before and after work hours and even during vacations. In the twenty-first century, everyone (even those in nonmanagement positions) seems to be overworked, running ragged to keep up with heavy workloads and short turnarounds.

Unfortunately, leaders who are constantly working lose perspective and burn out. They place excessive demands on their staff and have unreasonable expectations. As a result, workplace morale is low; many mistakes are made; distrust is prevalent; productivity is poor; and employees are stressed out, fearful, and difficult to retain and manage. Employees do not even get a respite when overworked bosses are away from the office, as these leaders check in by e-mail or phone.

Another, and most important, casualty of overworking is the executive's personal life. For every high achiever, there is a patient and supportive family member (e.g., spouse, partner, parent, child) who has been overlooked or a personal pursuit (e.g., hobby, advanced degree, creative aspiration, church involvement) that has been pushed aside. Over the long run, this situation could result in resentment at best and family and social breakdown at worst.

A new school of thought argues that maintaining a work–life balance has become a fallacy in a deadline- and travel-intensive global market. What matters, according to this theory, is the flexibility to respond to both work and life demands and an awareness of the consequences when one is chosen over another. In this sense, work and life are integrated, not separate entities that do not meet. That said, leaders should learn ways to cope with the demands of both work and life with the goal of doing their best at these two components.

Exhibit 9.2 offers strategies for pursuing or maintaining career success without sacrificing personal interests.

Exhibit 9.2 Practical Tips for Pursuing Work and Life

Minimize meetings. Many meetings are often unnecessary. Before you attend or host one, ask the following questions:

• What is the goal of this meeting?
• Can this goal be achieved without my presence?
• Can this goal be accomplished through other means, including e-mail exchanges or memos?
• What work could I do if I do not attend this meeting?
• Could I delegate attendance to this meeting to someone else?

Prioritize work and life to-dos. First, write two comprehensive lists—one for work, one for personal. Second, categorize items on both lists as urgent (U), important (I), or can wait (CW). Third, assign an order to the items in each category (1 for first to be done, 2 for next, and so on) according to level of importance. Such a priority list serves as a visual reminder and as a stress reducer because the items are part of your daily functions, not just weighing on your mind.

Allow for regular downtime. Schedule a block of time every week, for at least two to three hours, to get away from job stressors. Even if you cannot physically leave the workplace and stop all tasks, take time out to tend to low-pressure activities. Some executives take one or two days away from the office every couple of months to regroup. Unplugging from wireless devices or smartphones (the "crackberries," as they have been called in the media) for at least several hours a day is also a wise move.

Be flexible with time. A tight schedule does not allow for the surprises inherent in healthcare operations. The same is true for personal life. Being flexible does not mean ignoring the calendar altogether, but it does mean having a willingness to accommodate unplanned or unforeseen demands, whether they are work- or home-related.

(continued)

(continued)

Get regular exercise. Regular physical activity boosts energy levels and helps clear the mind.

Volunteer. Giving back to the community not only enhances your reputation but also gives you fresh perspectives. Join the board of a local service organization, participate in fund-raising activities, or perform outreach work for a cause you would like to advance. Volunteering is an ideal activity in which to involve your friends and family.

Find an Enjoyable Outlet

Healthcare pushes many of its executives to the limit. Many leaders are fatigued, are tapped out, and want to change careers.

An undertaking that has nothing to do with the field can refresh a leader who is suffering from burnout. It presents opportunities for developing out-of-the-box solutions and stimulates thinking. It also hones teamwork and learning skills as well as the leader's humility, as he is now a follower instead of the main person in charge.

Simply spending time with family and friends can be an enjoyable outlet.

Show Initiative

The greatest proof of a leader's commitment is her initiative. Initiative is the drive to chart a new direction with no outside encouragement or command. Some healthcare leaders define initiative as follows:

- "Doing more than is required—going the extra mile."
- "Actively seeking out issues and problems."
- "Being proactive, not reactive."

- "Engaging in positive thinking."
- "Not being a minimalist."
- "Avoiding the negativity of blaming others and acting like a victim of circumstances."

Only by taking the initiative can you follow your own course. As the Spanish poet A. Machado writes, "Wanderer, there is no path. You lay a path in walking."

Be Prepared to Make Sacrifices

Leadership expert John C. Maxwell has said, "Sacrifice is a constant in leadership. It is an ongoing process, not a one-time payment." The advice "you must pay your dues" is often given in healthcare, which is primarily hierarchical in structure. As such, the expectation is that those interested in moving up the organizational ladder need to yield to the demands (and politics) of their position, investing much energy and time in their projects and performing work that no one else opts to do. For example, new health administration program graduates are assigned tasks, such as copying and cold calling, that do not require an advanced degree. Similarly, middle managers are sent out to attend time-consuming, low-level meetings or to handle face-to-face patient complaints. The purpose of these seemingly menial assignments is not to punish the staff members but to test their team orientation, "get-to-it-tiveness," and commitment to their careers.

Making sacrifices, however, is not confined to non–senior management staff. Executives are also expected to make concessions for the good of the enterprise or the team. Over time, such sacrifices build up, giving the executive a bank of goodwill that can be drawn on when needed.

In a way, making sacrifices is an American value because it is based on the principle of "hard work merits rewards." The

> Subordinates often become committed to goals simply by seeing the sincere and enthusiastic commitment of top leadership to them.
>
> — **Richard Hughes, Robert Ginnett, and Gordon Curphy (2009)**

American public generally scoffs at people who rely on their good fortune, not years of honest efforts and even failure, to become successful.

Think Positively

Positive thinking is a deliberate act, a choice that can be made in the face of negative scenarios. It transforms bad attitude and victim mentality, and it overtakes people's tendency to fear the worst. Committed leaders make a conscious decision to think positively and have a good attitude because they want their initiatives to succeed. Even when an effort is, by all indications, going to have less-than-optimal outcomes, committed leaders dwell on the bright side—that is, they look for lessons, instead of mistakes. Mistakes have a negative connotation that makes people wary and defensive. Lessons, on the other hand, focus on improvement and development.

Positive thinking has its share of detractors (most recently, well-known author Barbara Ehrenreich), who contend that it shields us from reality and thus sets us up for disappointment. This cynical view, however, breeds bad attitudes that only perpetuate the difficulty of any situation and weaken commitment.

Be Mindful of Body Language

A leader's body language and facial cues communicate many messages. For example, an executive's frown as he paces the hallway could signal stress, while his warm smile and leisurely walk may represent his approachability. Commitment (or lack of) can be displayed through body language as well. Uncrossed arms, eye contact, leaning slightly into the other person, and standing or sitting to be equal in height with that person are just some examples.

Promote Employee Participation

As discussed in Chapter 8, ensuring staff satisfaction is no longer enough; leaders must also encourage employees to take part in organizational efforts. One way to support this idea is to delegate responsibility to staff.

Many healthcare workers, including managers, are highly reliable and intelligent. They await an opportunity from their superiors to use their skills and judgment on an important initiative. Such an assignment contributes to the employee's sense of commitment to her job and to the organization, not to mention to the process and outcomes of the project or task.

This manager–worker connection could inspire other involvement, including that of physicians, patients, and families. Lastly, employee engagement could increase morale and help in the recruitment and retention of high performers. Exhibit 9.3 enumerates the contributors to employee engagement.

Exhibit 9.3 Organizational Factors That Contribute to Employee Engagement

Excellent organizational reputation. Highly engaged employees are found in organizations known for providing high-quality care and other public services to their community.

Clear job expectations. Highly engaged employees know exactly what their roles, responsibilities, and goals are.

Close relationships with supervisors. Highly engaged employees report to managers who leverage the staff's individual capabilities and meet their professional needs.

(continued)

(continued)

Regular feedback. Highly engaged employees receive frequent comments on their individual and team performance for the purpose of learning and improvement.

Recognition and celebration. Highly engaged employees appreciate rewards and celebrations for their efforts.

Career advancement/continuous education. Highly engaged employees are encouraged to pursue educational interests and in-house promotional opportunities.

Develop an Organization System

Being organized is a symbol of being committed. It signals that the leader is always in control of her time, tasks, and priorities, among other things. Such a leader uses all available tools, such as filing systems, calendars or planners, and smartphones. A personal assistant assists the leader in managing her schedule.

CONCLUSION

To committed leaders, work is not drudgery or toil; instead, it offers great satisfaction. In the classic book, *The Seven Habits of Highly Effective People*, Stephen Covey (1990) lists being proactive as the first habit. According to Covey, being proactive is a function of commitment and work ethic. Now, imagine an organization teeming with proactive workers and leaders, then realize that your organization can become one, too. As the saying goes, "Practice makes perfect."

∗ ∗ ∗

———————— Self-Evaluation Questions ————————

* What does commitment mean to me?
* Am I paying a price for the work I do? Is that price worth the rewards I am receiving? Do I enjoy my work?
* What does "paying dues" mean to me?
* If my staff were to describe my facial expressions at work, what would they say?
* To what degree am I organized? Do I regularly run behind schedule? Do I keep a daily/weekly to-do list and accomplish most, if not all, of it?
* Consider the following quote from Katzenbach and Smith (1993). To what extent does this description apply to my contributions to the team?

> Team [members] work hard and enthusiastically. They also play hard and enthusiastically. No one has to ask them to put in extra time; they just do it. No one has to remind them not to delegate jobs to others; again, they just do the work themselves. To outsiders, the energy and enthusiasm levels inside teams are unmistakable and even seductive.

SUGGESTED READINGS

Catano, V. M., M. Pond, and E. K. Kelloway. 2001. "Exploring Commitment and Leadership in Volunteer Organizations." *Leadership & Organizational Development Journal* 22 (6): 256–63.

HR Magazine. 2006. "Exercise May Have Job-Related Benefits." *HR Magazine* 16: 6–7.

Ingersoll, G. L., J. C. Kirsch, S. E. Merk, and J. Lightfoot. 2000. "Relationship of Organizational Culture and Readiness for Change to Employee Commitment to the Organization." *The Journal of Nursing Administration* 30 (1): 11–20.

Judge, T. A., and J. E. Bono. 2000. "Five-Factor Model of Personality and Transformational Leadership." *Journal of Applied Psychology* 85 (5): 751–65.

Meyer, J. P., T. E. Becker, and C. Vandenberghe. 2004. "Employee Commitment and Motivation: A Conceptual Analysis and Integrative Model." *Journal of Applied Psychology* 89 (6): 991–1007.

Podsakoff, P. M., S. B. MacKenzie, and W. H. Bommer. 1996. "Transformational Leader Behaviors and Substitutes for Leadership as Determinants of Employee Satisfaction, Commitment, Trust, and Organizational Citizenship Behavior." *Journal of Management* 22 (2): 259–98.

Rode, J. C. 2004. "Job Satisfaction and Life Satisfaction Revisited: A Longitudinal Test of an Integrated Model." *Human Relations* 57 (9): 1205–30.

Whitener, E. M. 2001. "Do 'High Commitment' Human Resource Practices Affect Employee Commitment?" *Journal of Management* 27 (5): 515–35.

Case and Exercise

Case 9.1

Children's Hospital has a reputation for having the lowest turnover rate among the six hospitals located in the area, despite the fact that its average wages are approximately 10 percent lower than those offered by its competitors. In addition, Children's Hospital has the highest rate of employee engagement. Interestingly, University Hospital, which provides the largest compensation and benefit packages in the area, has the highest rate of turnover and the lowest rate of employee engagement.

Dori Shimbuku, a human resources consultant hired by University Hospital to study its recruitment and retention patterns, comes to the conclusion that University employees, including its leaders and managers, lack commitment.

Questions

1. What does Dori mean? What should she recommend University Hospital to do to enhance employee and leadership commitment?
2. How might commitment be measured?

Exercise 9.1

Several websites discuss employee engagement. Choose two of them and develop a presentation that answers the following questions:

1. What are the primary causes of high employee engagement?

2. What is the relationship between an employee's level of engagement and his/her relationship with his/her boss?
3. What practices should senior leaders develop to build employee engagement in their organizations?

The following links may be useful for this exercise:
- http://gmj.gallup.com/content/102496/where-employee-engagement-happens.aspx
- http://employeeengagement.ning.com
- www.fastforwardblog.com/2010/01/04/employee-engagement-a-core-goal-of-enterprise-2-0-adoption
- www.leadershipadvantage.com/organizationperformance/employeeengagement.html
- www.management-issues.com/2007/3/8/opinion/employee-engagement-what-exactly-is-it.asp

CHAPTER 10

Emotional Intelligence

During lunch at an off-site leadership seminar, a group of middle managers from the same health system participates in an open dialogue about the vice presidents in their institution.

Kyla: The strongest of the group is Melissa Varga. Her departments meet budgets year in and year out. Their clinical outcomes are high, and their retention is great. I'd like to work for that vice president.

Andrew: Well, I do work for her and I wish I didn't. Melissa is an emotional roller coaster. Some days she is calm and some days she just seems crazed. Behind closed doors, she is not beyond using threats to get us to achieve our goals but often what all of you see is this calm and controlled leader. She is far from that. We are expected to work many hours, and she is always frowning when we take vacation. My department is all work and no play. We are really stuck with her because she has all the clinical departments reporting to her.

BJ: I heard she throws tantrums. I was going to apply for a job working for her, but someone warned me. I'm glad to work for Mike Randolph. This guy is one cool cucumber. He constantly gets things done and does not get overexcited when things go wrong. He is thankful to us and respects all our work, so we respect him back. He has a very good sense of interpersonal skills and can control his emotions. Even under pressure, he does not lose his composure.

Kyla: He sounds like a robot, but better than Melissa, it seems. What's the difference then—they actually both achieve high results?

Andrew: Both of them are pretty strong execs. The difference is emotional intelligence.

BJ: What's that?

Kyla: It means the person has a good grasp of his or her emotions and feelings and how those are displayed externally. Leadership is not all about getting results. It's getting results without emotional outbursts or allowing anger to take over.

IN THE LATE 1990s, writer Daniel Goleman popularized the concept of emotional intelligence, setting off further inquiries into the relationship between feelings and intellect. Two pioneers of emotional intelligence are researchers Peter Salovey and Jack Mayer (1990), who define the term as follows:

> Emotional intelligence is the subset of social intelligence that involves the ability to monitor one's own and others' feelings and emotions, to discriminate among them and to use this information to guide one's thinking and actions.

Emotional intelligence has two components: energy and maturity. Energy (or the spark or zeal for life) refers to the liveliness and stamina with which people approach their work. It keeps leaders fresh and motivated when others have had enough and are ready to give up. Maturity, meanwhile, refers to people's refinement, social graces, tact, capacity to grow and change, and ability to interpret signals from others. It reminds leaders to apologize, express gratitude, harbor no ill will, empathize, have a sense of humor, and respect others. Also, maturity keeps leaders poised during times of distress and wise during times of pressure. Although maturity is often associated with old age, it can be learned at a young age.

> Your first and foremost job as a leader is to take charge of your own energy and then to orchestrate the energy of those around you.
>
> —Peter Drucker (1997)

Emotionally intelligent leaders make every effort to develop their leadership skills, knowledge, and abilities. They also work hard to be aware of their inner emotional self and the world around them. They are confident, are enthusiastic, and have self-esteem and a positive attitude. They discern nuances in (and thus are sensitive to) people's words and actions. They are aware of the effect that their (and others') needs, beliefs, motivations, and feelings have on their surroundings. They know how damaging passive-aggressive behaviors and one-upmanship can be in the workplace. They are watchful of situations where they and others deal with conflict, criticisms, stress and pressure, and difficult people. They use a "self-awareness lens" that enables them to see the communication and behavioral patterns that showcase the worst in people, including themselves.

Simply put, emotionally intelligent leaders have a robust capability for reading people and receiving and giving critical feedback. This ability comes from their firm understanding of their own and others' feelings and the environment in which they operate.

THE SELF-AWARENESS FACTOR

In the book *Emotional Intelligence at Work*, author Hendrie Weisinger (1998) sets out the following steps to improving emotional intelligence:

1. Develop high self-esteem.
2. Manage your emotions.
3. Motivate yourself.

4. Develop effective command skills.
5. Develop interpersonal expertise.
6. Help others help themselves.

According to Weisinger, self-awareness is the main driver of these steps. Self-awareness is a universal panacea for negativity and enables leaders to

- accept (even anticipate) constructive criticism;
- avoid feeling defensive;
- support those around them;
- be assertive but not aggressive;
- have confidence in their ability to initiate change;
- view scenarios as "win–win";
- not be hostile, overbearing, or impatient; and
- take charge of situations.

Conversely, leaders who are not self-aware misinterpret events and other's comments, throw tantrums or act out, and are reactive rather than proactive.

Many executives, because of their high rank, have become so removed from daily operations and staff that they do not even realize how others in the organization perceive them. When in the office, they primarily deal with their direct reports, a group that mainly consists of other senior managers who are likely also isolated from staff. As a result, their workplace reality becomes distorted and their emotional intelligence dulls.

Worse, their self-awareness is based on incomplete information or incorrect assumptions about others' assumptions.

THE CONCEPT IN PRACTICE

The following principles can enhance emotional intelligence.

Develop Personal and Social Competence

Experts suggest that emotional intelligence may be managed through learning and improving both personal and social competencies. Personal competence includes such attributes as self-awareness, self-control, and self-motivation. Social competence, meanwhile, includes social awareness, empathy, collaboration, and teamwork. This concept is explained by Kavita Singh (2010):

> In order to connect the individual has to bring into play certain personal, social and organizational competencies in mutually acceptable combinations for achieving organizational excellence…. Personal competencies play a very vital role in influencing the emotional intelligence of employees in organizations.

Characteristics of Emotionally Intelligent Leaders

Comfortable and self-aware. They are confident with their skills, goals, and visions but value continuous improvement. Thus, they welcome feedback.

Reflective listener. They show a genuine interest in other people and their ideas. They encourage others to lead discussions or give input. They rarely interrupt, preferring instead to wait their turn.

Nonthreatening and nonintimidating. They are open and approachable. They do not use power to manipulate their followers, and they are aware that the trappings of their high rank are easily misunderstood and could corrupt their reputation.

Available. They avoid appearing constantly busy as it signals that they do not highly regard the everyday tasks and challenges of employees. They invite others to speak with them directly, and they attend events of great importance to staff.

Seek Feedback

Emotionally intelligent leaders do not feel threatened by feedback, whether from direct discussions or through 360-degree assessment tools. These executives relish the chance to receive ratings and comments from peers, subordinates, and other associates because they understand the role of feedback in their personal and professional development.

Appendix B presents the Emotional Intelligence Questionnaire, a tool that leaders can use to obtain direct feedback. This instrument seeks participation from staff and associates at all levels of the organization to ensure comprehensive results. To ensure confidentiality of the feedback, the tool discourages participants from sharing their comments. For the best outcome, a neutral third party should administer the tool, collate comments, and provide a full report to the leader being evaluated.

Set a Personal Path and Follow It

Many individuals possess little sense of personal direction, especially those who get caught up in the busyness of daily operations. These leaders are effective in establishing and monitoring organizational objectives, but they do fall short when it comes to their own career.

Emotionally intelligent leaders frequently take stock of where they have been and what they have accomplished. They know their long-term and short-term personal goals and seek to work in organizations that provide opportunities for fulfilling those goals. In other words, they look for fit between their personal mission and the organization's mission so that both entities can benefit from the union. For example, an individual who intends to make a difference in the public health system will not be served well by working in a large for-profit organization. Some emotionally intelligent leaders weigh their career options by occasionally interviewing for open positions even when they do not intend to leave their jobs. This exercise allows them to compare their skills and accomplishments with current standards and expectations.

Leaders who are not attuned to their personal intentions or path can more easily get derailed by the unceasing demands of healthcare management.

View Annual Retreats as a Time for Self-Reflection

Most members of religious orders and some lay persons often take religious retreats. These are planned getaways, which last for a few days to a week, that focus on intense introspection. Although these retreats are intended to reconnect participants to their original aspirations, some people go a step further: They reflect on their own strengths and weaknesses and incorporate their abilities into their leadership style. One nun admitted to designing a succession plan while on a retreat.

Get a Coach

Executive coaching has become one of the fastest growing areas of consulting, as executives have realized the benefits of having a neutral advisor. These coaches can assess current behavior, management style, and performance; offer unbiased feedback; and teach practical skills for improvement and for managing perceptions. In addition, coaches are helpful in establishing a clear career vision or direction.

Many emotionally intelligent leaders rely on their coaches, with whom they discuss private details of their jobs and from whom they seek counsel. The book *Exceptional Leadership* presents a detailed guide on how to use executive coaches (Dye and Garman 2006, 213–18). Several coaching websites also offer information on this topic—see, for example, www.theexecutivecoachingforum.com, www.coachfederation.org, and www.coachnet.com.

Manage Your Emotions

Managing emotions is not the same as lacking emotions. In a world of social networking where sharing personal information and reactions has become routine practice for everyone who has an account, it is easy to assume that those who maintain composure have no feelings or are "robots." Emotionally intelligent people do, in fact, have lots of emotions—only they tend to show positive feelings such as optimism, sympathy, and confidence, not defeat, anger, or vengeance.

Emotionally intelligent leaders know that positive messages are influential. They inspire followers, and they keep them enthused about initiatives, even the difficult ones. Negative emotions, on the other hand, are not motivational. They instill fear and anxiety, and they could erode trust and respect.

Executives do reach points at which their frustrations take over, a natural occurrence in management. Over time, these emotional outbursts could escalate and turn into an angry personality that the person does not even see. Cursing, shouting, namecalling, chronic complaining, and impatience are some signs of poor emotional control. Emotional intelligence expert Hendrie Weisinger (1998) notes that physiological changes can be observed in people who "lose their cool," so to speak, including heart palpitations, perspiration, and rapid respiration.

Although emotions are a natural response to everyday stimuli, they can become detrimental in the workplace if they are not appropriately showcased. Leaders should watch out for their personal emotional triggers (and the responses described by Weisinger) in an effort to slow down or transform their reactions.

Expect Setbacks

Leaders respond to setbacks differently. Because they are more optimistic, emotionally intelligent leaders cope well with challenges. Some of these leaders take a mental or physical break from the activity and return with renewed commitment, while others view setbacks as a personal test they must pass. In an effort to better deal with setbacks, one CEO carries around a laminated card with the following message:

> You will get knocked down at times.
> You will taste dirt occasionally.
> But it is through this process that
> You will better enjoy the return to the air above.

Maintain Physical and Mental Health

Healthcare is physically and mentally exhausting work, even for those who do not provide direct care. As such, healthcare leaders must maintain their health, which enables them to be of service to their staff and patients. A good amount of rest, sleep, and exercise and a balanced diet go a long way toward this wellness. A regular visit to the doctor, vacations or time off, and a stress-decreasing routine also help.

The point is that leaders who are too tired or too physically and mentally run-down are ineffective, negative, and short-tempered. They are not approachable, and they behave unpredictably, to the detriment of the employees and the organization. Emotional intelligence cannot be developed and sustained in an unhealthy mind and body.

CONCLUSION

Emotional intelligence is more critical today given that the command-and-control style of leadership is no longer the norm. More and more healthcare leaders understand that they have to earn, not expect, respect and trust. Being emotionally intelligent is one way to practice this understanding. Emotionally intelligent leaders do not use their power to gain an advantage over others; are aware of their intentions, accomplishments, and shortcomings; manage their emotions; and welcome feedback. This level of maturity requires a lot of work, something that an emotionally intelligent leader strives toward.

―――――――――― Self-Evaluation Questions ――――――――――

* How isolated have I become from direct personal feedback?
* How well do I know myself?
* Would others say that I am plagued by frequent bouts of emotional inconsistency, such as outbursts of anger, hostility, or antagonism?
* How do I manage my emotions?

SUGGESTED READINGS

Emmerling, R. J., V. K. Shanwal, and M. K. Mandal (eds.). 2008. *Emotional Intelligence: Theoretical and Cultural Perspectives.* Hauppauge, NY: Nova Science Publishers.

Gardner, W. L., D. Fischer, and J. G. Hunt. 2009. "Emotional Labor and Leadership: A Threat to Authenticity?" *Leadership Quarterly* 20 (3): 466–82.

Marques, J. F. 2007. "Leadership: Emotional Intelligence, Passion and…What Else?" *Journal of Management Development* 26 (7): 644–51.

Nelis, D., J. Quoidbach, M. Mikolajczak, and M. Hansenne. 2009. "Increasing Emotional Intelligence: (How) Is It Possible?" *Personality & Individual Differences* 47 (1): 36–41.

Stein, M. 2005. "The Othello Conundrum: The Inner Contagion of Leadership." *Organization Studies* 26 (9): 1405–19.

Case and Exercise

Case 10.1

Mike Sebastian has been the director of facilities for more than 30 years. Up until the past three years, the facilities department had low turnover. Today, however, the turnover rate is at 30 percent, causing concern for Rena Shah, the chief human resources officer at the hospital.

To understand the problem, Rena pays a visit to several of Mike's former employees.

First worker: I retired because of him. I couldn't take the constant panic he gave me. He wasn't that bad when he first started—a little temperamental but nothing to complain about. But he changed a lot in my last years there. He would lose his top when he found out something was not done or someone made a complaint about us. It was hard to live with.

Second worker: I quit six months after he hired me. Mike was a screamer. People outside the department didn't know because he seemed great with everyone else. Behind closed doors, though, he could dress you down. No job was worth that. Even though I needed the money and was really looking forward to being eligible for the pension plan, I decided to leave for my own peace of mind.

Third worker: Forget about talking to him! He would never listen. He's old school. He thinks it's his way or the highway. I once tried to reason with him to calm down the situation, but he fired me. And I put in the best five years of my life in that job. With all due respect, Ms. Shah, you should give him the boot and give him a taste of his own medicine.

Questions
1. How should Rena address the problem with Mike?
2. What do you think triggered Mike's transformation in the last three years?

Exercise 10.1
As mentioned earlier, emotional intelligence may be managed through learning and improving both personal and social competencies. Personal competence includes self-awareness, self-control, and self-motivation. Social competence, meanwhile, includes social awareness, empathy, collaboration, and teamwork.

Go to the website of Consortium for Research on Emotional Intelligence in Organizations (www.eiconsortium.org) and develop a list of the specific leadership behaviors that characterize emotional intelligence. How do these behaviors match up with your own?

PART III

TEAM VALUES

CHAPTER 11

Cooperation and Sharing

The professor opens his class with a question, "As you know, I do a lot of executive team building and executive coaching with senior leaders across the country. What do you think is the greatest challenge in getting senior executives to work together in a collaborative and cooperative way?"

His students volunteer the following responses:

- Most of them don't have the time to be part of a good team.
- A lot of their work takes place outside the team with other teams and groups of people.
- A group of executives does not fit well into a team. They have to follow what the CEO says, and they really do not have that much say in their activities.
- At that level, there is more interest in who gets the credit for the job.
- They are not really all equals. Probably the CFO or the CNO or someone like that is really viewed at a higher level than the others. Without equality, you cannot get a team to work.

The professor replies, "Those are all good thoughts! The real challenge, from what I have experienced, has been participation—that is, active participation. If all the team members participate, then I can help them build an atmosphere of sharing. That is when the team becomes focused on shared goals and mutual trust."

TOO MANY MEETINGS today have a hypnotizing show-and-tell style: One by one meeting attendees tell the others about their project and show (with PowerPoints and handouts) how the project is progressing. Questions and answers are volleyed, but often very little attention is given to identifying the problems that could arise, or have arisen, from the undertaking. No one asks about the details of or the reasons for the project, and few volunteer their help. At the end of these meetings, people file out no less removed from others' projects. Consequently, when successes or failures happen they become an individual's accomplishment or failure, rather than a team celebration or setback.

Although the healthcare industry prides itself on emphasizing individual authority and accountability, it should also support and encourage team dynamics because building teams means encouraging efficiencies.

Teams are predestined for failure when they lack the fundamental values of teamwork—cooperation and sharing. Both elements require team members' willingness and the team leader's encouragement and support. Simply, cooperation and sharing demand that team members sacrifice some of their individuality for the benefit of the entire team.

THE CONCEPT IN PRACTICE

Strengthen your team with the following strategies.

Build the Right Team from the Start

Most CEOs who come into an organization rebuild all or at least part of their executive team. They do this for two reasons: (1) to establish their "mark" on the organization and (2) to assemble a team of people who espouse similar values. Most executives who are tapped to become part of the new team are excited about the opportunity.

Often, this excitement translates to wanting to share and cooperate.

When recruiting, leaders must consider people who believe in the concept of teams. They should evaluate prospective members with the following guidelines:

1. Ask prospects to recount an actual situation in which they worked with a team and by doing so developed a solution that was much better than their own. Listen carefully for the candidate's inclination—or disinclination—toward teamwork and behavior.

2. Ask prospects to recount an actual situation in which they had problems working with teams. Ask them how they handled their frustration.

3. Ask prospects to describe a situation in which team efforts do not work very well.

4. Ask prospects to name the values that drive effective team interaction (see Chapter 15).

5. Administer a validated personality assessment, such as the Hogan Personality Inventory, to assess the prospect's personality and leadership style and how she would support effective team interaction.

6. When speaking to references, ask specific questions about team behavior. Ask references to describe how the prospect gets along with fellow team members. Ask for examples of how the prospect argues or debates issues during team sessions. A good

Team effort enhances...

Coordination and reduces bureaucracy. Assigning specific functions to people helps eliminate overlapping responsibilities, duplication of duties, and red tape.

Involvement and support. Because everyone works together toward a common goal, the focus shifts from receiving personal glory and recognition to supporting the team's objectives and valuing the contributions of others. "That's not my job" is replaced by "It's all of our jobs."

General oversight and reduces problems that "fall through the cracks." Everyone is involved in making sure that nothing is overlooked or undermined.

The joy of celebrations. One of the reasons sports bind people is everyone enjoys watching the exhilaration of team victories. An accomplishment is always grander when more people share and enjoy it because it represents the combination of each person's hard work, sacrifice, and dedication.

Creativity. When more people are involved various perspectives and new ideas are generated and better results are achieved.

idea is to ask the extent to which the prospect "plays politics" among fellow team members.

Discuss with the Team Its Value and Values

All team members should learn their individual roles and expectations, evaluate their personal worth to the team, and participate in establishing the values that drive team interactions and behavior. Doing so improves relationships and cooperation. Because team members are often so busy with their own daily activities, they fail to invest the necessary time to fully grow and develop as a unit. The team atmosphere should encourage spirited, but respectful, debate because better decisions emerge through this exchange.

Under an autocratic CEO, open discussion is unlikely to occur. Teams under such a leader are formed merely to fulfill an organizational convention. Members cannot, nor know how to, partake in actual decision making. As a result, members are not aware of their roles and importance. Of course, the underlying problem in this scenario is the leader; however, such a team can be salvaged by a new leader, who can ingrain the values of teamwork with constant dialogue and team exercises.

Demonstrate the Value of "Teaming"

Team leaders must involve all members in setting achievable short-term goals. Achievement of these goals demonstrates the team's value and contribution to improving the organization. An effective leader can demonstrate the value of teaming by bringing tough issues to the group and asking every member to suggest solutions and alternatives. Too often, leaders prefer to handle especially difficult problems themselves or to delegate them to a small subset of the senior management team. Exhibit 11.1 lists strategies for increasing team member participation.

Determine the Purpose of the Team

Unfortunately many teams do not know why they exist. When asked, most teams respond with "We share information" or "We

---

Exhibit 11.1 How to Increase Team Participation

Establish a clear connection between the team's purpose and activities and the organization's mission and vision. Members need to know not only what they are doing but also how their individual tasks tie in with the bigger goals.

Forge personal relationships with members. Genuine camaraderie is built on members' familiarity with each other's personal interests and pursuits.

Allow and encourage informal discussions (e.g., dialogue about children, movies, or personal interests) before or after team meetings. Occasionally, food may be brought in or the group could conduct the meeting over an off-site lunch.

Reward and recognize hard work and accomplishments. A portion of the organization's incentive program should be allotted for team bonuses. If this is not an option, the team leader should plan and provide some other form of celebration.

Make team decisions within the confines of team meetings. Members must be present during deliberations and when a final decision is made; merely announcing the decision to the team will harm team morale and discourage future involvement of its members.

Treat all members equally. No one member should be a favorite, regardless of how frequently that person volunteers and how much that person contributes to the team function.

Several years ago, I led a senior management team retreat. Before the retreat, I met individually with team members to ask them the following questions:

- What are the primary reasons for the existence of this senior management team?
- What are the primary reasons for the meetings of this senior management team?
- Does the content of the meetings support the primary reason for the existence of the team?

The responses were varied, but most members indicated that their reason for being was to "collectively lead the organization."

During the retreat, it was revealed that team meetings were show-and-tell sessions, not the mutual interaction that members envisioned. This revelation led to an in-depth discussion about the need to (1) shape and follow a clear purpose and (2) restructure meeting patterns. The team decided to meet every other week solely to discuss strategy and to meet weekly to discuss day-to-day operations.

This team, save for a few members who left to pursue other opportunities, remains intact today. The members report being closer and managing conflicts more effectively.

discuss strategy," while some say (perhaps mistakenly) "We run the organization."

Ideally, the team, as a unit, should determine its purpose; however, the leader could establish it as well. This purpose provides a framework for what the team must accomplish, so it must be clear and must be understood by every team member. Clarity of purpose prevents the team from taking on activities and goals (or prospective members) that are vague or inappropriate.

Engage in Team-Building Exercises

Any exercise that confirms the collective strength of the team, assesses the dynamics of the team, and aids in the interaction among members is beneficial. Common team exercises range from simple personality assessment tools (e.g., Myers-Briggs Type Indicator, Hogan Personality Inventory) to extensive physical activities (e.g., Outward Bound).

These exercises offer practical knowledge and skills in a fun and relaxed environment. One note of caution is in order: The person who plans these activities must be an expert on the method, team building, and the objectives the team is trying to attain; otherwise, the program could become an expensive time waster for all involved.

Confront Relationship and Conduct Issues

Conflicts between team members should be expected. Sometimes such clashes require the leader to intervene, such as when they create disruptions in team functioning. Other times, however, the team itself will police behaviors, discuss ways to stem the conflict, and dole out appropriate punishment if necessary.

Developing a team code of conduct is a valuable team-building exercise. Not only is this activity cooperative, it also delineates the rules that protect members and monitor their behavior and interactions. Many senior management teams work together on a team code of conduct during their retreats. Exhibit 11.2 is an example of team conduct expectations; this code has been adopted by many healthcare organizations and is currently used by a Midwestern health system.

Exhibit 11.2 Example of a Senior Management Team Code of Conduct

- Each of us has a right to her/his own opinion and has the right to state it. Each of us expects that others will carefully and respectfully listen to our opinion and seriously consider it before rejecting it.
- Although our CEO has the authority to make unilateral decisions, he will engage all of us in giving input in as many issues as possible. We respect his right to "some days count the votes and some days weigh the votes."
- We recognize that some decisions are better made with subsets of our team. However, except in unusual situations, we agree that these decisions will not be finalized until the entire team is notified and has the chance to provide final input.
- Each of us has the right to campaign for our issues outside of team meetings and meet individually with other team members to petition for support. However, we agree to tell the team that this campaigning has been done.
- Mystery, intrigue, and politics are fatal diseases. We will strive for openness, honesty, and tact.

Match Words with Actions

The organizational team structure is one way an organization can respond quickly and adapt to constant and rapid changes in workplace conditions.

—Peter G. Northouse (2004)

A team leader's words and actions carry greater weight than those of members. As such, the leader has to ensure that her behaviors are consistent with her messages, and both must be consistent with the organization's mission, vision, and values. Any discrepancies that team members observe could, at best, become fodder for gossip and, at worst, weaken the trust and respect that the leader worked hard to establish. Worse yet, it could decimate the participative way of the team, with members perceiving that the leader only preaches about cooperation and sharing but does not really practice these team concepts.

Even in informal interactions, the leader must be watchful of his body language and casual banter to ensure that he remains appropriate, professional, and a role model for others on his team.

One of the most classic examples of how **not** to be a leader is Nathan Jessup, the fictitious well-decorated lieutenant colonel played by actor Jack Nicholson in the 1992 movie *A Few Good Men*. Here is how Colonel Jessup defends his leadership:

> I have neither the time nor the inclination to explain myself to a man who rises and sleeps under the blanket of the very freedom I provide, then questions the manner in which I provide it! I'd rather you just said thank you and went on your way.

Although Colonel Jessup has achieved much, he is not someone a team will choose as, or be proud to call, its leader.

Challenge the Current Boundaries

The hierarchy in every organization creates boundaries, including the following (Band 1994):

- Boundaries of authority—who is in charge of what?
- Boundaries of task—who does what?
- Boundaries of politics—what is our payoff?
- Boundaries of identity—who are we as a group?

Although boundaries are necessary, they can impede decision making and workflow. The leader must allow team members to challenge these boundaries when necessary by setting "must" (critical) and "should" (recommended) guidelines. For example, the team *must* first gain approval from department directors before implementing a process, but the team *should* include all levels of employees in decision making. In this way, the team knows which boundaries are off-limits and which are flexible. To promote cooperation, one leader told his team: "I expect all of you to work together as though you had authority over the entire organization. Leave your claims of functional turf at the door."

CONCLUSION

Decision making, problem solving, brainstorming, planning, and implementation are activities that are most effective when executed by a team, not by one person alone. Cooperation and sharing are team traits that do not happen without an open dialogue among team members and without support from the team leader.

* * *

—————— **Self-Evaluation Questions** ——————

* Has my team ever discussed its purpose?
* Do my team members truly believe in the value of teams? The value of team deliberations?
* Does my team regularly participate in team-building activities?

SUGGESTED READINGS

Frisch, B. 2008. "When Teams Can't Decide. Are Stalemates on Your Leadership Team Making You a Dictator by Default? Stop Blaming Your People—Start Fixing the Process." *Harvard Business Review* 86 (11): 121–26.

Garman, A. N., K. D. Fitz, and M. M. Fraser. 2006. "Communication and Relationship Management." *Journal of Healthcare Management* 51 (5): 291–94.

Miles, S. A., and M. D. Watkins. 2007. "The Leadership Team: Complementary Strengths or Conflicting Agendas?" *Harvard Business Review* 85 (4): 90–98.

Schaubroeck, J., S. S. K. Lam, and S. E. Cha. 2007. "Embracing Transformational Leadership: Team Values and the Impact of Leader Behavior on Team Performance." *Journal of Applied Psychology* 92 (4): 1020–30.

Cases and Exercises

Case 11.1

Malcolm Holcomb is the new CEO at a medical center. The agenda for his first meeting with the senior management team includes the following questions:

- What has been the primary purpose of the senior management meetings in the past? What was discussed? What was accomplished?
- What do you want to be the primary purpose of these meetings moving forward? What should we discuss? What should we accomplish?
- What meeting format do you prefer? Do you think that format will enable us to better meet our goals?
- Do each of you have a clear understanding of your roles? Do each of you help one another? How much cooperation and sharing should we expect from this team?

Questions

1. You are one of Malcolm's vice presidents. How would you answer these questions?
2. Should Malcolm discuss these questions privately with each senior management member *prior* to raising them in the full group (and

therefore getting more open feedback than in an open meeting)? If so, how should he proceed after these private meetings?

Case 11.2

Cynthia Jonas is the CEO of a large suburban community hospital. Her senior leadership team is made up of 17 people, 5 of whom report directly to Cynthia and the rest report to the chief operations officer. Every Tuesday, the entire 17-member team meets for two hours, and often the meetings run longer by about another hour.

During the meeting, Cynthia gives a summary of all the meetings she attended in the prior week. Then, she turns to the chief medical officer (CMO) to discuss physician issues and to the chief financial officer (CFO) to discuss the budget. During these conversations, no one else but Cynthia poses questions and comments to the CMO and the CFO. The rest of the group stays silent or prepares their own report.

By the time Cynthia ends her conversation with the CMO and CFO, only 15 to 30 minutes are left. The team then goes around the table to give their respective department or project updates. Most team members use this time to tout their accomplishments, but no one pauses for congratulations or recognitions, as time is running out. During these updates, Cynthia is on her laptop, checking e-mail or answering correspondence. Occasionally, she asks for clarification or offers advice.

Recently, Cynthia hired Luann Crosby, an executive coach. Luann sat through one of these meetings. Afterward, Luann pulled Cynthia aside.

Luann: You know there's a problem with that meeting, right?
Cynthia: What do you mean? They're a little long, but no one complains about them.

Exercises

1. You are Luann. Give Cynthia an extensive diagnosis of the meeting. Include as many details in your diagnosis as possible.
2. Give Cynthia specific recommendations on improving the meeting.
3. How will you get Cynthia to buy into your suggestion? How will you coach her to gain buy-in from her team?

CHAPTER 12

Cohesiveness and Collaboration

At a focus group during a leadership conference, Rakesh Jaya, the facilitator and organizational development researcher, asked participants from different organizations to explain the structure and results of their own senior management meetings.

James Smith, chief operations officer: All of our meetings are preplanned and highly structured. We do not meet unless there is a clear reason for it. We follow the agenda strictly and honor the time allotment for each agenda item. A detailed follow-up list is prepared at the conclusion of every meeting. Everyone is required to come well-prepared for his or her reports and to participate in all the discussions.

Elizabeth Rodriguez, chief executive officer: Our team meets every two weeks, and the meetings last for four to six hours. Long ago, the team collectively decided that we will not use an agenda because it is too limiting. Our meetings are open-ended, so we have the freedom to explore and deliberate on an issue fully. We arrive at many of our decisions this way, and we think this is a creative approach to thinking about and resolving our problems. We realize that this structure is not for everyone, so only the senior-level members of our team are invited to the meetings. But we do provide a summary of our discussions to the rest of the team, and they are encouraged to speak to their vice presidents if they have any concerns or comments.

Amy Broderick, chief financial officer: I work for a large system, and our team is composed of 25 members. Every week, the chief executives from our nine hospitals meet for two hours to discuss strategic issues. Each of these meetings is focused on one issue and is led by a sponsor. This way, all team members have an opportunity to run a meeting and be well-informed about at least one strategy. Then every month, the entire 25-person team meets to exchange reports about business unit outcomes, ongoing and upcoming strategic initiatives, and some operations-related issues. If needed, we invite staff outside of the team to provide input and share information.

Steve Michael, senior vice president of communications and marketing: We built subgroups into our team to increase our efficiency and effectiveness. The subgroups meet every week, and they report their discussions and decisions to the full team when we all meet twice each month. Our CEO trusts our judgment and skills, so she gives us much autonomy but expects us to be accountable for our outcomes. Before the start of our monthly meeting, we open with a breakfast and the CEO says with a huge smile on her face, "Tell me something I don't know," then people start talking about their children's wedding or a movie they just saw. There is always an opportunity for us to get to know each other in a more personal way. We all know and respect each other, and I think that because of that we offer help to those who are struggling with their operations or projects.

MANY LEADERSHIP TEAMS in healthcare strive to capture the entrepreneurial spirit of successful businesses. This spirit makes a team cohesive, as it cheers team members on through conception, development, rollout, and marketing of new products or services. Unfortunately, this spirit is temporary and can be undermined by old-fashioned jealousy and selfish tendencies.

When a business expands its operation, new members are added to the existing team. Although a logical move, this addition could be destructive to the cohesiveness of the team, as current and new members feel tension or quarrel over whose idea is better, who has the power to make decisions, who is responsible for which tasks, or what improvements need to be pursued (or not pursued). As the rift grows, member support for the common goal diminishes. Although cohesiveness increases team productivity, morale, and camaraderie, it does not prevent schism brought on by territorial battles and other issues. Exhibit 12.1 lists the downsides to cohesiveness.

Exhibit 12.1 Disadvantages of Team Cohesiveness

Low performance norms and poor performers. Performance norms are the standards expected from all team members. They dictate the quality and quantity of work—how vigorous, effective, and productive the work is; what goals should be achieved; and what contributions should be tendered. In a cohesive environment, these norms (primarily unwritten) are low. Highly competent members pick up the slack (perhaps even gladly) for members who have subpar abilities. As a result, those who need skills improvement remain undeveloped and dependent on the high achievers. In a contentious environment, however, low performance norms become a source of conflict. The best performers resent the fact that they have to cover for the poor performers. Worse, many competent members are too polite to deliver constructive criticism.

Proliferation of groupthink. Groupthink is, simply, unanimous thinking. When the team is cohesive, its members tend to lose their individual perspectives. As a result, new and creative thoughts are blocked off, objections are stifled, and concurrence becomes the standard. Instead of pursuing the goals of the organization as a whole, keeping the solidarity of the team becomes the team's main purpose.

Low tolerance for change. Founding team members are loyal to the initial team purpose, composition, rules, norms, and goals they helped establish. They believe that these components strengthen team cohesiveness, which is given high value. As such, they are uncomfortable with change, even when they recognize that evolution could improve team functions. New members are often viewed as disruptive outsiders and detrimental to the cohesiveness of the team.

(continued)

(continued)

Team goals take precedence over organizational goals. A highly cohesive team is fanatical about the welfare of its members. Some leadership teams have reduced clinical and support staff but maintained administrators. Some have paid executive bonuses despite financially tight years, a practice that has gained significant public disapproval.

Collaboration, on the other hand, pulls together divided parties to work toward a mutually accepted goal. It transcends traditional compromise in that no exchange of services is necessary to achieve the preferred outcomes of both parties; it demands only equal input and dedication to the cause. Most important, collaboration often results in conflict resolution.

Conflicting parties typically respond in one of the following ways:

- Avoid the other party and thus the conflict
- Give in to the demands of the other party
- Compete with a goal to win
- Compromise or strike a deal
- Collaborate with a goal to achieve

Consider the last three approaches. Competition is never an appropriate response because it amplifies the damage and makes it irreversible. Historically, compromise was often recommended, but it leaves both parties only partially satisfied and distorts the quid-pro-quo practice of "saving" favors (see Chapter 13) to be redeemed in a later conflict. If neither party anticipates future dealings with one another, then a compromise is usually a better approach than collaboration. Conversely, if the parties continue their relationship and expect further dispute, then collaboration is the only responsible solution. This is the case with senior leadership teams.

Cohesiveness begets collaboration, and collaboration begets cohesiveness. Although one can exist without the other, one cannot be as effective without the other.

THE CONCEPT IN PRACTICE

Despite its disadvantages, cohesiveness is an important component of collaboration. The following methods can help in forming a cohesive and collaborative team.

Minimize Selfish Behavior

In teams, selfishness is a contagious disease that can easily spread to all members. The team leader, as the role model, must demonstrate that she works on behalf of others' interests, not just her own. If not, team members will suspect the leader's motives and cohesiveness will decline. The leader is also responsible for confronting members who contribute only to advance their own pursuits, not the team's. Appropriate team behavior must be established and put in writing—possibly during a retreat (see discussion about team code of conduct in Chapter 11).

> **What Is Groupthink?**
>
> • An illusion of invulnerability, which leads to unwarranted optimism and excessive risk taking by the group
> • Unquestioned assumption of the group's morality and, therefore, an absence of reflection on the ethical consequences of group action
> • Collective rationalization to discount negative information or warnings
> • Stereotypes of the opposition as evil, weak, or stupid
> • Self-censorship by group members from expressing ideas that deviate from the group consensus due to doubts about their validity or importance
> • An illusion of unanimity such that greater consensus is perceived than really exists
> • Direct pressure on dissenting members, which reinforces the norm that disagreement represents disloyalty to the group
> • Mind guards who protect the group from adverse information
>
> **Source:** Information from Hughes, R. L., R. C. Ginnett, and G. J. Curphy. 2009. *Leadership: Enhancing the Lesson of Experience*, 6th edition. Columbus, OH: McGraw-Hill/Irwin.

Assess the Size of the Team

Mergers and acquisitions, new service lines, and corporate partnerships extend the reach of an organization's leadership team and expand its size. As new members and responsibilities are added, the team loses its camaraderie and cohesiveness. A team that has more than 11 or 12 members often experiences a split, whereby the members form their own factions because they cannot find a commonality among the entire group. Another problem with a large team is that the members do not receive enough individual attention.

The generally accepted principle is that the team should have between 6 and 11 members. However, there is no ideal size. Here are several important considerations for setting the team size:

- If the task is repetitive, the team may have many members.
- If the task is complex, a large team can slow down the decision-making process.
- If a lot of collaboration is required, teams larger than 11 or 12 members can create problems.

If reducing the team size is not an option, the leader could manage perception about the size through the following approaches:

- Divide operations and strategy executives into two teams.
- Hold less frequent meetings with the entire team, but convene subgroups more often.
- Do not replace a team member when turnover occurs.

Get to Know One Another

Team leaders should socialize with members at every opportunity presented, including before or after meetings, organizational events, and informal celebrations. These interactions not only create a personal bond between the leader and members but also communicate that the leader is interested in the person behind the executive.

Consider the following bonding practices by several successful leaders:

- Every fourth Friday, one CEO takes her senior management team to an off-site location for a full-day retreat. The first half (from breakfast until lunch) of the retreat is dedicated to business and operations. The second half is reserved for non-work-related matters, such as getting-to-know-you exercises.

- After its monthly meeting with the board, one leadership team spends the day at an off-site location to enjoy each other's company and catch up. The different venue serves to refocus the team and inspire creativity.
- One CEO holds a weekly no-agenda lunch session with his team, allowing team members to interact with one another in an informal setting.

Minimize the Influence of Cliques

Unfortunately, cliques are not confined to junior high school; they are prevalent in the workplace as well. The larger the organization, the larger the teams; the larger the team, the greater the possibility of cliques forming. Cliques are detrimental to any team because they represent cohesiveness without collaboration. That is, they are powerful because of their solidarity and focus on a common goal, but they fail or even refuse to partner with others to achieve that objective. Thus, they alienate others and disrupt the normal function of a team.

The leader can address the challenges of cliques within the team in several ways:

1. *Occasionally acknowledge the clique's existence during team meetings.* For example, one CEO announces (only half jokingly), "I already know that the operations people have come to a conclusion on this matter a long time ago. Now I want to know what they talked about before this meeting!" By publicly recognizing the clique, the leader is making it clear that side negotiations will not be tolerated.

2. *Confront the clique privately.* Generally, a clique engenders negativity among team members because it has its own agenda. Divide and conquer could be one of the approaches a clique can use to sway the opinion of team members who are unde-

cided about a certain decision or plan. By confronting the clique, the leader is directly appealing to its sense of propriety while strongly emphasizing the need to work together, not sabotage, team efforts. This confrontation must be done calmly so as not to widen the rift between the team and the clique.

3. *Assign clique members to a task force related to their area of expertise.* The goal of this strategy is to capitalize on the clique's strengths to benefit the team. Many members of a clique are experts in their field, and they withhold this knowledge from the team to further their own agenda. If the leader delegates them to a task force specific to their areas—for example, clinical quality improvement task force—clique members are more likely to apply their skills and abilities and teach other team members.

4. *Have an open discussion with the entire team about the damage a clique, or any subgroup, can inflict on cohesiveness and collaboration.* Such a discussion (which is a good topic for a retreat) is sensitive and should be done with an expert facilitator.

Discuss and Evaluate the Team's Purpose

Over time, the team's composition changes. As old members leave and new members take their place, the team's reason for being evolves as well. The team must regularly (annually, perhaps) redefine its purpose, reassess its goals, and reestablish its expectations. This discussion must involve all team members, as nothing inspires commitment more than 100 percent participation from those who will embody the principles and implement the changes.

Treat All Members Fairly and Equally

Imbalance of power produces divisiveness, which is counter to the ideas of cohesiveness and collaboration. The fact that some members fill higher positions or have more organizational and community clout than do the rest of the team should not affect the way the leader regards all team members.

For example, if two members (say, the chief operations officer and the chief nursing officer) commit the same indecent behavior (say, sexual harassment), the leader cannot excuse one but sanction the other. Not only will this action spark a protest among the team, but it will also run counter to the service mission of both the team and the organization. The same can be said for personal relationships. The leader cannot pick and choose which member he will befriend or get to know better. Doing so will send a message that the leader plays favorites and will cause team members to distance themselves.

> Cohesiveness 'is the sum of forces that attract members to a group, provide resistance to leaving it, and motivate them to be highly active in it.'
>
> —Richard L. Hughes, Robert C. Ginnett, and Gordon J. Curphy (2009)

Designate a Team Role for Each Member

A team role is a specific character or function that each member consciously or unconsciously inhabits at any team gathering (e.g., meeting, retreat). Roles include cheerleader, devil's advocate, team conscience, team historian, and meeting planner. A member's personality or professional background lends itself to role assignment. For example, a member who has worked for the organization for 30 years could be named the historian.

Although seemingly simple, the practice of role designation reinforces members' sense of belonging to the group and clarifies their contributions.

Reassess the Compensation Policy

The organization's compensation structure indirectly affects team cohesiveness. That is, if the pay policy is designed primarily to recognize and reward individual performance, the message is that team participation and outcomes are not as valued. As a result, team members may reserve their best work for their own individual projects (the accomplishment of which will yield a bonus or raise) or develop hidden agendas that could conflict with the team's. Although compensation is beyond the purview of this book, it is an important consideration for the leader.

Rally the Team

As detailed in chapters 1 through 3, today's executives are faced with multidimensional and interrelated challenges. The most difficult times are always the most opportune times for the leader to pull the team together, especially if the team has experienced infighting and division.

Rallying the team should go beyond vocal cheerleading to boost morale, however. It should be backed up by practices that ease conflict and promote unity. For example, at the end of every meeting, the leader exclaims, "We're a great team! Let's get those quality numbers up!" However, at the next meeting, the leader publicly berates one group for the poor outcomes it achieved while exalts another group for its remarkable performance. Worse, he does not offer guidance or advice to those who are struggling. This leader's mixed message facilitates unhealthy competition, retards collaboration, and discourages improvement. At the end of the day, team members will only hear "we're a great team!" but not believe in it.

CONCLUSION

Without cohesiveness and collaboration, a team is merely a collection of people who sit around a conference table when they are told to do so. Such a team produces nothing without difficulty and waste, which in turn cascade to the rest of the organization. More important, this kind of team does not advance the mission and vision of the organization nor meet the needs of the community it supposedly serves.

* * *

———————— **Self-Evaluation Questions** ————————

* Why does my team meet? What do we accomplish when we meet?
* Would outside observers describe my team as cohesive?
* Has my team studied collaboration? Have we had training in conflict resolution?
* Consider the symptoms of groupthink listed earlier in this chapter. What symptoms does my team exhibit?

SUGGESTED READINGS

Cohn, K. H. 2008. "Collaborative Co-Mentoring." [Online article; retrieved 07/26/09.] healthcarecollaboration.com/collaborative-co-mentoring.

Frisch, B. 2008. "When Teams Can't Decide. Are Stalemates on Your Leadership Team Making You a Dictator by Default? Stop Blaming Your People—Start Fixing the Process." *Harvard Business Review* 86 (11): 121–26.

Miles, S. A., and M. D. Watkins. 2007. "The Leadership Team: Complementary Strengths or Conflicting Agendas?" *Harvard Business Review* 85 (4): 90–98.

Schaubroeck, J., S. S. K. Lam, and S. E. Cha. 2007. "Embracing Transformational Leadership: Team Values and the Impact of Leader Behavior on Team Performance." *Journal of Applied Psychology* 92 (4): 1020–30.

Case and Exercise

Case 12.1

St. Nicholas Health System is an integrated health delivery organization comprising St. Nicholas Medical Center, Suburban Western Health Center, Suburban East Health Center, the St. Nicholas Employed

Physician Practice, St. Nicholas HMO, and St. Nicholas Home Care and DME Corporation. The health system operates in a highly competitive city of 2.5 million residents.

Headed by CEO Elizabeth Parris, the leadership group has 25 members, including the executive vice president and chief operations officer (EVP/COO), several system senior vice presidents, assorted system vice presidents, and the site administrators from each business unit.

The senior team meets weekly to discuss tactical and strategic operations as well as ongoing projects (if time allows, which is rare).

The site administrators do not feel they are part of the executive team, given that they report to the COO and not to the CEO and that most of the discussions relate to the system rather than the individual business units. In fact, at St. Nicholas, much of the work is accomplished through interactions between the vice presidents or executive directors and administrators or middle managers. Because Elizabeth is a hands-off leader, she has given her EVP/COO freedom to make ongoing operations decisions. The EVP/COO gives the site administrators much autonomy to run their own facilities.

Elizabeth depends heavily on only three executives on the team—the EVP/COO, the senior vice president of medical affairs, and the chief financial officer. The rest of the 25-member team is aware that Elizabeth has frequent daily communications with these three executives.

Questions

1. What are the strengths of this team? Its weaknesses?
2. Do the site administrators belong to this group? Explain your answer.
3. What message does Elizabeth send to her team by relying so much on three team members over everyone else?
4. If you were a consultant, what advice would you offer Elizabeth to strengthen the team?

Exercise 12.1

Some leadership experts argue that members of the senior management team independently work on their own issues and come together only occasionally to coordinate organizational activities and set organizational strategy.

Consider the following thoughts regarding the work of senior leaders and their teams:

1. The job of a typical healthcare vice president has an individual focus. That is, he spends most of his time on activities that have nothing to do with the work of the senior management team of which he is a member.

2. Working challenges faced at the middle management and first line supervisory level are usually short term in nature (there is an immediacy to the nature of the issue), and the problems that must be solved are usually clearer. Issues at the senior management level are much grayer, involving strategy and longer-term decisions.

3. Compared with the problems faced by middle management, the challenges encountered by the senior management team require strategic (not operational), long-term responses. Similarly, the purpose of a senior management team (e.g., achieve a 4 percent margin) is more abstract than the purpose of any other organizational teams.

4. Senior-level leaders have two, often overlapping, performance goals—corporate and individual.

5. At the senior leadership level, complementary skills are less important than position. In true team situations, the extra performance capability that a real team provides comes mostly from its complementary skills—that is, executives with clinical backgrounds are knowledgeable about patient-care operations, while leaders with financial backgrounds are adept at business concepts.

6. Establishing and maintaining team standards of behavior are difficult for a senior management team because this group meets less frequently than do other teams.

7. Members of senior management teams are not "mutually accountable" to each other; rather, they are individually accountable to the CEO. Mutual accountability is hard to establish because one executive has too many responsibilities.

Questions

1. If these points are correct, how should senior executives enhance their working effectiveness? Can executives create real teams?

2. If you were starting an organization from scratch, how would you assemble the leadership team?

CHAPTER 13

Trust

Major Michelle Harris, an Army Medical Service Corps officer, has just returned to the States from a third deployment in Iraq. As a healthcare executive, she is active in her professional association's local chapter. In one meeting, she and her fellow executives discuss the concept of trust in leadership.

Chuck: Michelle, in your position, it must be great to simply give orders that your team will not question or distrust. I would love to do the same in my hospital. But I have to sell every idea, earn my colleague's trust every step of the way.

Michelle: No, that's not how it works in the military. There is a book called *Leadership Lessons from West Point*. It points out that in the military, trust is even more critical than in civilian situations.

Chuck: How so?

Michelle: In the military, we ask—note that I say "ask" not "command"— people to put their lives on the line, so we work harder to earn their trust. We provide constant training to ensure high levels of competency and safety. We demonstrate that we care about our personnel, and a high degree of openness can be observed in our training. We have to be on the same page, especially in combat situations. Everyone has a deep understanding of our missions and the dangers and payoffs they present. The movies about the military do not accurately depict the high levels of trust that underlie everything we do.

Chuck: That's quite impressive. I'd like to invite you to speak to my senior management team next week, if you have time to spare.

TRUST IS THE first value all team members must learn. Without trust, team members engage in fierce competition, back stabbing, and hypocrisy (see Exhibit 13.1).

Merriam Webster's Collegiate Dictionary defines trust as the "assured reliance on the character, ability, strength, or truth of someone or something." In leadership teams, trust is the members' confidence in each other's ability and resolve to uphold the team's principles and to work toward its goals. It is what allows one member to vote for another's untested, seemingly outlandish proposal. It is what makes members stand behind their leader in moments of failure or scrutiny. Exhibit 13.2 enumerates the essential bases of trust, and Exhibit 13.3 is a behavior guideline for all team members to promote a culture of trust.

In teams, an exchange of tangible or intangible favors or goodwill is common practice among team members. This transaction is

---

Exhibit 13.1 Consequences of a Lack Trust

- Team members keep important and relevant information to themselves for fear that others will steal or sabotage their ideas.
- The team leader and/or high-ranking team members undermine the suggestions or plans submitted by lower-level members.
- Competition for resources among team members is excessive.
- Side deals or negotiations constantly occur.
- Many team members are deliberately left out of the planning and decision-making processes.
- Cliques have more influence on and power over team members than does the leader.
- Political maneuvering is rampant and viewed as a necessary practice.

---

modeled after the economics of bartering or the social exchange theory, which posits that individuals decide the fairness of a relationship on the basis of a self-measured give–take ratio. If a person thinks he is giving more than he is receiving, he will perceive the exchange as unfair, and thus he may withdraw from giving. Conversely, if the person believes the things he gives and receives are of comparable

---

Exhibit 13.2 The Five Components of Trust

1. *Integrity*—honesty and truthfulness
2. *Competence*—technical and interpersonal knowledge and skills
3. *Consistency*—reliability, predictability, and good judgment
4. *Loyalty*—willingness to support, protect, and save someone else
5. *Openness*—willingness to share ideas and information freely

Source: Information from Robbins, S. 2005. *Essentials of Organizational Behavior,* 8th edition. Upper Saddle River, NJ: Prentice Hall.

Exhibit 13.3 Role of Team Members in Engendering Trust

Speak your mind. The truth could hurt, but it could also pave a path for better and more communication. Be calm while you express yourself, and be receptive to the responses.

Maintain confidentiality. A lot of leadership team matters are confidential, and for good reason. Such matters, including informal or casual conversations, must not be discussed or shared.

Actively support the team. Do not refer to or speak about the team negatively, inside or outside the team setting. People's poor perception of the team extends to their poor perception of you, if only because you belong to the group.

Embrace openness. An open and candid environment develops trust.

Practice due process. Within the team setting, due process means that all team members have the right to be heard fairly.

---

value, he will continue the exchange relationship. The same idea is true of trust. It is a commodity that team members can exchange.

Unlike other favors, however, trust is not easily earned. A team member must prove her trustworthiness to the rest of the group by showing and having faith and concern; being transparent and accountable; providing support, assistance, information, and resources; and aligning with the general consensus without sacrificing personal values. More important, the team member must display these behaviors consistently and over time.

Once earned, trust must be maintained.

When team members cease to trade trust, a "depression" occurs, prohibiting members from cooperating, sharing information, and collaborating. It harms the cohesiveness of the unit and ultimately leads to various dysfunctions.

THE CONCEPT IN PRACTICE

The following approaches can enhance trustworthiness and trust levels among team members.

Acknowledge the Quid Pro Quo Practice

Honesty engenders trust. By publicly recognizing and discussing the fact that favors are exchanged to help forward the team's initiatives, team members can learn how to use that fact to achieve the most optimal outcomes. The concept may be woven into trust-building exercises.

Earn, Not Expect, Trust

Trust does not develop overnight, especially in an industry that is in a constant state of flux. A leader cannot order her team members to trust her, nor can she think that trust comes automatically with the position. She must first assess her true self and either improve or maintain her trustworthiness. Trust building is a multistep and multiyear journey that can be easily derailed by a small move in the wrong direction.

An understanding of people and relationships requires an understanding of trust. Trust requires the coexistence of two converging beliefs. When I believe you are competent and that you care about me, I will trust you. Competency alone or caring by itself will not engender trust. Both are necessary.

—Peter R. Scholtes (1998)

Display Consistent Behavior

In some respects, trust is about predictability and consistency. Team members will be hard-pressed to have confidence in a leader who does not do what he says or is fickle, temperamental, indecisive, impulsive, or too spontaneous. Also, followers are discouraged when the leader's words and deeds are contradictory. For example, one CEO declares that he wants to create a culture of empowerment, but he insists on reviewing everyone's work all the time and giving the final approval on every single decision. An erratic or unpredictable leader is viewed as unreliable, hence not deserving of trust.

Drive Out Fear

In *Beyond the Wall of Resistance*, author Rick Maurer (1996) writes that "the opposite of trust is fear." He believes that the absence of trust starts a pattern of fear that escalates to resistance to change. As resistance increases, people become polarized and trust decreases further.

Clearly, fear has no place on any team. Following are some strategies for driving fear away:

- Establish and sustain a culture in which people can express opinions, concerns, suggestions, and even dissent without putting their jobs, reputation, undertaking, or team membership in jeopardy.

- Do not discuss or negotiate anything in secret. Confidentiality is markedly different from secrecy, and the latter breeds suspicions, gossip, and disloyalty. Secrets are always revealed, and when they are, team members feel left out and threatened. Everyone on the team must practice transparency.
- Persuade members to participate in team activities. One leader holds "Think Out Loud" meetings, where the team brainstorms ideas. The goal of this session is to stimulate creative thinking and generate novel approaches to old challenges.
- Be accessible. The executive suite should not be a hiding spot; it should be one of the places a leader can be found, in addition to the hallways, patient care units, conference rooms, cafeterias, other people's work spaces, and so on. Presence at organizational events and community functions as well as the availability of contact information are two of the ways a leader can become more accessible.

Avoid the Perception and Reality of Conflict of Interest

Many situations in healthcare present a conflict-of-interest challenge because healthcare delivery and management entail so many types of exchanges, some of which could work in the self-interest of those involved in the exchange.

Full disclosure is one way to combat the perception of a conflict of interest. For example, the Cleveland Clinic now publicizes the business dealings of its physicians and other clinicians with drug and medical device makers. In April 2009, the Institute of Medicine issued a report—*Conflict of Interest in Medical, Research, Education and Practice*—that states: "Disclosure by physicians and researchers not only to their employers but also to other medical organizations of their financial links to pharmaceutical, biotechnology, and medical device firms is an essential first step in identifying and managing conflicts of interest and needs to be improved" (IOM 2009).

Many healthcare organizations, including professional associations and healthcare businesses, already have a conflict-of-interest policy in place. However, more needs to be done in this area to minimize (if not eliminate) the risk of conflict of interest and its subsequent consequences to the reputation of the organization, its leaders, and its staff.

Be Candid

Candor is the sincerity and frankness of speech and behavior. It prevents a person from lying, condescending, or exaggerating.

Speaking candidly means

- retaining eye contact and a steady voice;
- stating facts, and withholding opinions that could hurt;
- focusing on the situation, and not going off on a tangent;
- inviting questions or comments; and
- giving the other person a chance to respond.

Retreats are optimal moments for candid discussions, as John Kotter (1996) proposes in his book *Leading Change*: "Most of the time must be spent encouraging honest discussion about how individuals think and feel with regard to the organization, its problems and opportunities. Communication channels between people are opened or strengthened. Mutual understanding is enlarged. Intellectual and social activities are designed to encourage the growth of trust."

Unfortunately, many team members recoil from voicing their opinions and concerns in front of the whole team, as my experience with leading senior management retreats has shown. Although these members were willing to be candid with me (in private), they preferred not to speak when

> Trust in a relationship generally develops gradually over time through the course of personal interaction. Taking some kind of risk in relation to the other person and feeling you weren't injured (emotionally or physically) in the process is what moves trust to new levels.
>
> —James Kouzes and Barry Posner (2002)

faced by the other members. To combat this phenomenon, I started meeting individually with team members before the retreat. I emphasized the merits of being open and honest, and I recruited them to contribute to the group dialogue. Also, I occasionally brought a list of concerns, with permission from the team, to serve as a starting point for our candid discussion.

Finesse does not cost anything, but it is worth a small fortune. However, like a battery, finesse is negatively and positively charged. Dealing with someone with decorum and courtesy is a plus, but it can also be a minus: It can prohibit confrontation needed to reveal underlying conflicts. For example, a cohesive leadership team that has been together for many years and has rarely argued over issues does not take kindly to confrontation. As suggested in Chapter 12, a cohesive team does not necessarily make a productive team because many of its members have grown complacent; thus, the team can use a little shake-up once in a while. Having tact, however, prevents anyone from boorish behavior.

Expect and Welcome Resistance

The process of earning trust—essentially, being open—puts a person in a vulnerable position. The leader (or a team member) should be prepared for criticism, doubt, resistance, and reluctance but should not take these responses personally. One CEO puts this in perspective: "If you want trust within your management group, you have to expect to get shot down sometimes. Then you get back up, thank the person who shot you, and move on."

Do Not Take Advantage

A leadership position offers many opportunities for inappropriate conduct. Sadly, in the past decade alone, high-level executives in and out of the healthcare industry have exploited this truth. Taking advantage for the purpose of personal gain is wrong in any situation, as this act almost always has a victim. A leader could keep herself from taking advantage by obeying the golden rule of bartering: The exchange must be of equal value.

Grant Authority Appropriately

The power to bestow decision-making capabilities on team members falls on the leader, so he must exercise extreme care and judgment. Personal friendships, resentment or anger over past insults, and even lack of information can cloud the leader's ability to grant this authority. A poor choice can lead to infighting, charges of favoritism, and resistance. It could also erode the leader's trustworthiness. The best defense against such a scenario is always awareness and wisdom, which can come from being fully present physically, mentally, and emotionally.

Understand the Links Between Trust and Mission and Action

As the vignette indicates, military operations exemplify how trust is the basis of mission fulfillment. Trust essentially powers the actions that support the mission. Without trust, the action either does not occur or is performed haphazardly, causing grave harm. As Major General David Rubenstein, FACHE (2009), states:

> The first thing that comes to mind when talking about trust is the chain of events that occur in the Army from

words to actions to trust to mission accomplishment. A soldier will hear his or her leader's words but waits to see the leader's actions. When action matches words the soldier starts to build a trust that says, "I'll go in harm's way to do my job, because I trust you." When I hand my static line to the jumpmaster, 800 feet above the ground on a moonless night, I'm saying, "I'm ready to jump out of this plane because I trust you've ensured that I and my equipment are ready."

CONCLUSION

Trust is the assurance of goodwill between two people. It builds over time and must not be taken for granted. Trust among team members is a commodity that can be traded, facilitating ongoing relationships and improving the likelihood of collaboration, cooperation, and sharing of information.

Lacking trust is like walking into a room full of complete strangers. You have a problem: You need to finish an important project, but you have no time to do so. Imagine asking these strangers in the room to help you. Imagine handing them the incomplete work. Imagine sharing with them valuable and confidential information about the project. Imagine encouraging them to collaborate and cooperate with each other. Imagine giving them a quick deadline. Imagine doing all of this without feeling paranoid, doubtful, desperate, exasperated, and doomed.

* * *
—————————— Self-Evaluation Questions ——————————

* How is trust displayed among my team members? Do we barter trust, and do we understand its function within the team?
* Is my leadership style marked by openness and honesty? Do others easily approach me?

* To what extent am I known as a good team player?
* Is my communication with the team candid and straightforward? To what extent do I encourage this communication style?

* * *

—————————— **Team Evaluation Questions** ——————————

To what extent does the team
* believe in each member's abilities and competence?
* believe in each member's inclinations and intentions?
* believe in each member's integrity?
* get along with each other?
* share the same goals?
* rely and depend on each member?
* have confidence in each member's motives and behavior?

SUGGESTED READINGS

Avolio, B., and W. L. Gardner. 2005. "Authentic Leadership Development: Getting to the Root of Positive Forms of Leadership." *Leadership Quarterly* 16 (3): 339–40.

Burgoon, J. K., and D. B. Buller. 1994. "Interpersonal Deception: Effects of Deceit on Perceived Communication and Nonverbal Behavior Dynamics." *Journal of Nonverbal Behavior* 18: 155–84.

Gilbert, D. T., R. W. Tafarodi, and P. S. Malone. 1993. "You Can't Not Believe Everything You Read." *Journal of Personality and Social Psychology* 65: 221–33.

Pfeffer, J. 1992. *Managing with Power: Politics and Influence in Organizations.* Boston: Harvard Business School Press.

T³ Group. *Trust: Theory and Technology.* See www.istc.cnr.it/T3/index.html.

Vogus, T. J., and K. M. Sutcliffe. 2007. "The Impact of Safety Organizing, Trusted Leadership, and Care Pathways on Reported Medication Errors in Hospital Nursing Units." *Medical Care* 45 (10): 997–1002.

Cases

Case 13.1

New CEO Doug Wright has a problem. His leadership team displays dysfunctional behaviors. Infighting is rampant, and cooperation and sharing of information are nonexistent. At meetings, most team members do not participate in the discussion, resigned to sitting quietly after they give an update on their respective responsibilities. Recently, two chief executives suddenly quit, leaving the other team members gossiping about the reasons.

Doug has spoken to the team, both as a group and individually, at length about the problem. He has touted the values of openness, honesty, and trust. He has encouraged the team to speak their minds and has informed them of the no-recrimination policy he has just instituted. But still, the team seems removed, content with doing as they are told.

Frustrated, Doug contacts Roxanne Samanski, an organizational development consultant. The first question he asks her is, "Shall I fire all of them and start fresh?"

Questions

1. If you were Roxanne, how would you respond to Doug? What suggestions would you offer?
2. What is the role of lack of trust in this situation?
3. Do you think it's important to find out the history of this team to understand its current dysfunctions?

Case 13.2

Ralph O'Riley is a dynamic CEO of a large for-profit system. He is well known in the community. He is a brilliant businessman, and he is highly rewarded for it, enjoying various perks such as a beautifully appointed office suite, a company car, and a parking spot right outside of the hospital entrance.

He rarely attends employee-related functions, and he only occasionally visits the other facilities in the system, let alone the units on his own campus. He is a mythical figure among employees and intimidates his own leadership team. He shows up to meetings late, relies on his chief executives to "fill him in on the agenda," and does not know all of his staff's names and their positions. He does not participate in operational discussions, but he gives orders that affect operations, something that confounds his team and angers employees.

Once during a retreat, he was overheard by some of his team members boasting about his golf game and his power: "This is a waste of my time," he complained over his cell phone. "It's not PC to say it, but I own these people. They do what I tell them to do. I made a lot of money for this system. Now they should give me a break."

Questions
Obviously, everything Ralph is seems to run counter with the practices that build and enhance trust.
1. What long-term effects does Ralph's behavior have on the team, the employees, and the organization as a whole? Are these effects irreversible?
2. Ralph is clearly a financial wizard and has great business instincts. How should he leverage these competencies to create a better culture? To make himself even more powerful by being approachable and trustworthy?
3. What role does power play in Ralph's success?

CHAPTER 14

Conflict Management

Newly hired Jack Lewis is a vice president of clinical quality and education. Among his many responsibilities are nursing education and supervision of the clinical nurse specialists (CNSs). During his orientation, Jack rotated through various patient care units, talking with the managers and staff about his goals for improved patient safety and a more comprehensive and coordinated nursing education program. Throughout his visits, he was well-received by all of the staff. One week after his visit to surgery, he received the following e-mail from Margaret Strong, the vice president of surgical nursing, who reports to Mike Volkman, the chief operations officer, not to Barbara Apolinario, the chief nursing officer who is Jack's boss:

Jack,

I appreciate your enthusiasm for nursing quality and education. I must tell you that surgical nursing is different from the rest of nursing at the hospital. Surgery does not have a need for your services. I have talked to Mike and Barbara, and it has been decided that the two CNSs who work in surgery will now be under my direct supervision effective immediately. Please do not plan any nursing education or quality improvement programs for surgery since we intend to plan our own. Thank you for your attention to this matter.

Margaret

CONFLICT IS THE natural byproduct of the human thought process. It is present within us and is exacerbated by our interactions. The workplace, especially where decisions are made and imple-mented, hosts various kinds of conflict. How big a conflict becomes and how fast it spreads depend on the number of people involved, the situation's degree of difficulty, and the power structure in place.

Healthcare management is a breeding ground for conflict, as its issues span from operational to strategic and all points in between and even beyond. Such conflicts require leaders to be engineers of con-sent. That is, they must invite others to suggest solu-tions, guide that discussion, build consensus, and manage the discord that arises.

A conflict management guideline will help the leader and man-agement team in this regard. Such a document, however, was shunned for years by many organizational leaders. They knew it was a critical instrument, but they offered myriad excuses for not cre-ating one, including lack of time and few incidents of conflict. Fortunately, in 2009, The Joint Commission issued a mandate: All hospitals and health systems must develop and put into practice a guideline for managing conflicts within leadership teams. Recognizing that leadership conflicts can endanger human lives, The Joint Commission states (Bricker & Eckler 2009):

Conflict commonly occurs even in well-functioning hospitals and can be a productive means for positive change. However, conflict among leadership groups that is not managed effec-tively by the hospital ... has the potential to threaten health care safety and quality. Hospitals need to manage such conflict so that health care safety and quality is protected. To do this, hos-pitals have a conflict management process in place.

HOW CONFLICT IS BENEFICIAL

Conflict is not fundamentally good or bad. After all, conflict represents our ability to reason, to work through a maze of possibilities and impossibilities. Also, it signifies the diversity of our perspectives, interests, and experiences. However, conflict can cause difficulty when it is not properly addressed.

In team functions, conflict also presents benefits, such as the following:

- *Ends complacency.* Conflict opens team members' eyes. They begin to see obstacles, inefficiencies, outdated practices, improprieties, and the like.
- *Starts dialogue.* Conflict almost always triggers a discussion—often heated and often generating more conflict. The once quiet majority (or minority) is now adding its voice to the conversation. Turns out, everyone has something to say.
- *Activates a plan.*
- *Forces participation.*

The ultimate problem with conflict is that it intimidates many people. Thus, it is seldom addressed—and inappropriately at that. Typically, minor conflicts—those that have no lasting implications—are ignored because they usually resolve themselves. However, over time, even minor conflicts (if persistent and repetitive) have the potential to turn major and corrupt and disrupt the team's performance and purpose.

THE CONCEPT IN PRACTICE

Following are strategies for preventing and responding to team conflicts.

Create a Conflict Management Policy

The first step toward conflict management is acknowledging that conflict inevitably occurs when intelligent, opinionated people converge. The second step is developing rules so if a conflict does occur, all members can debate, deliberate, and compromise accordingly. These rules should be reviewed regularly by all members, and new members must be informed of their existence. Exhibit 14.1 is an example of conflict management guidelines.

Exhibit 14.1 Conflict Management Guidelines

1. *Declare the conflict.* Not all discussions during group interaction are conflict oriented. When a struggle ensues, however, someone must inform everyone that a conflict has arisen so that proper procedures can be followed. Although this may sound trite, it can become a powerful tool for managing conflict appropriately.

2. *Give reason for the conflict.* Although disagreements and arguments are normal and necessary, they cannot be initiated out of caprice or malice. Strife, hostility, and animosity must still be avoided at all cost, but if they do surface the reason(s) must be stated.

3. *Clarify the issues of conflict.* A neutral group member or one who is not directly embroiled in the conflict must be elected to clarify contentions and interpret ambiguities. All members must actively participate in the dispute and specify in detail their issues. Although members are entitled to express their personal concerns or emotional responses, facts (not opinions) must govern the debate.

4. *Address one conflict at a time.* To ensure appropriate and thoughtful consideration of all issues, only one item at a time will be considered. Many people prefer to save their issues and raise them all during debates, but that practice should not be allowed or tolerated. All members should address their concerns as they occur.

(continued)

---

5. *All members must participate.* No party in the dispute will be allowed to "pull in his head" during the conflict. All must give their opinion and not cower behind others on their side.

6. *Be fair.* Members must keep their "weapons" appropriate to the level of the fight. In other words, no personal attacks are allowed in a strictly professional discussion, and each party is given an opportunity to respond to accusations and defend itself.

7. *Declare that the conflict is over.* All members must know that the debate has ended and an outcome has been reached. The outcome agreement should be specifically defined so that no confusion, which could escalate into another conflict, will arise later.

Root Out the Potential Causes of Conflict

Meeting format and length, team size and composition, and member assignments and responsibilities are petri dishes for conflict. The leader should observe these areas for potential and hidden troubles that render the team ineffective. For example, if the team meets too often, team members are not given the time to do their work. Similarly, if vocal members dominate every team discussion, the rest of the group will harbor resentment for not having the chance to talk, which will discourage their participation. See Exhibit 14.2 for more causes of conflict.

The point here is that a leader can be more proactive in managing conflict if she knows where it usually starts.

Adopt a Format That Works for the Team

Team members should help establish a format for the meetings. This way, they are more apt to uphold it. For example, each meeting is run by a team member, who also creates the agenda, invites

Exhibit 14.2 Reasons for Conflict

- Incompatible personalities or value systems
- Overlapping or unclear job boundaries
- Competition for limited resources
- Inadequate communication
- Interdependent tasks (e.g., one person cannot complete his assignment until others have competed their work)
- Organizational complexity (i.e., the greater the decision-making layers and special requirements, the greater the conflict)
- Unreasonable or unclear policies, standards, or rules
- Unreasonable deadlines or extreme time pressure
- Collective and consensus decision making
- Unmet expectations
- Unresolved or suppressed tension

Source: Information from Kreitner, R., and A. Kinicki. 1998. *Organizational Behavior*, 4th edition. New York: Richard D. Irwin.

guests if needed, distributes necessary materials before the meeting, leads the discussions, and so on. No matter the format suggested, the leader should make every effort to adopt one that promotes involvement, reduces cynicism, and benefits the attendees.

Practice "Directspeak"

Directspeak, a term I coined for speaking directly and clearly, is the straightforward manner of communicating without being insensitive. Directspeak does not work everywhere, but it thrives in team settings in which trust prevails because every member of these teams knows that confrontations are never meant to be personal attacks. CEOs or team leaders must be aware that some team members are uncomfortable with this technique, toe the line to avoid offending others, and are not active participants in debates. Conversely, some members are strong-willed and more verbal, which may intimidate the mild-spoken members. What results is another conflict: a personality conflict.

Management teams whose members challenge one another's thinking develop a more complete under-standing of the choices, create a richer range of options, and ultimately make the kinds of effective decisions necessary in today's competitive envi-ronments.

—**Kathleen Eisenhardt, Jean Kahwajy, and L. J. Bourgeois III (1997)**

Prohibit Personal Attacks

Strong personalities (and hence opinions) can usher in conflict. One way to minimize personality-induced conflict is to keep the discussion focused on the issues, not the people. The leader should step in when inappropriate comments are introduced. Spirited debates are invigorating, especially if they do not include personal attacks. When team members veer off the topic, one CEO gets up and jots down on the flipchart the goals of the discussion. His movement alone, not to mention that fact that he is pointing out the meeting's objectives, is often enough to rein in the chaos.

Insist on Collaboration

Chapter 12 lists the five usual reactions to conflict:

1. Avoid the other party and thus the conflict
2. Give into the demands of the other party
3. Compete with a goal to win
4. Compromise or strike a deal
5. Collaborate with a goal to achieve

These responses illustrate the sink-or-swim mind-set among team members.

Avoidance is valid only when the conflict is too minor to merit full-time consideration—that is, when the problem will resolve itself without intervention. Giving in or surrendering is tied to the system of bartering favors (see Chapter 13). Although well employed by teams, this system is a temporary fix and could lead to more conflict if not executed appropriately. Competition, sometimes called "forcing," creates an all-or-nothing environment in which members do everything possible to gain a win over their perceived enemies. In this sense, team meetings become a personal battlefield where members show off their achievement to gain more power. Compromise, while democratic, stalls conflict resolution because it relies on too many people and too many variables.

> Teams must agree on how they will work together to accomplish their purpose and goals. Real team members always do equivalent amounts of real work beyond and between meetings where things are discussed and decided. Over time, a team's working approach incorporates a number of spoken or unspoken rules that govern contribution and membership.
>
> —Douglas K. Smith (1996)

Collaboration bests all other responses. It is a mature approach, not merely a reaction, to conflict that yields long-term benefits. The leader should verbalize his support of collaboration and put in place goals and activities that require interdisciplinary partnerships.

Visualize the End of the Conflict

Conflict has a beginning. That's the bad news. The good news is it also has an end. By visualizing the ideal outcomes of a conflict, the team is also generating ideas to prevent and manage it. For example, if the desired or visualized outcome is regular and relevant communication between physicians (through the chief medical officer) and the C-suite, then the team could work backward, analyzing the causes of the conflict, brainstorming practical solutions, developing action steps, and assigning responsibilities for implementing those steps. Although conflicts do end, the end still has to be closely monitored to ensure that a conflict is not threatening to start again.

CONCLUSION

To a strong team, conflict is a temporary foe but a permanent ally. To a weak team, it is a predator. Regardless of its role, conflict is an inevitable occurrence in organizational life. Teams must understand that it is within their control.

✳ ✳ ✳

────────────── Self-Evaluation Questions ──────────────

* How does my team manage conflict? Is our approach working? If not, why not?
* What is my personal conflict-management style? Is it working?
* Does my team suppress conflict? Why?
* Has my team established a conflict-management policy? Was it developed for the team's sake, or to comply with requirements of The Joint Commission?
* How has conflict affected me personally?

SUGGESTED READINGS

Garman, A. N., D. C. Leach, and N. Spector. 2006. "Worldviews in Collision: Conflict and Collaboration Across Professional Lines." *Journal of Organizational Behavior* 27: 1–21.

Governance Institute. *Leadership in Healthcare Organizations: A Guide to Joint Commission Leadership Standards.* 2009. [Online information; retrieved 9/12/09.] www.jointcommission.org/NR/rdonlyres/48366FFD-DB16-4C91-98F3-46C552A18D2A/0/WP_Leadership_Standards.pdf.

Porter-O'Grady, T. 2004. "Embracing Conflict: Building a Healthy Community." *Health Care Management Review* 29 (3): 181–87.

Cases and Exercise

Case 14.1

Professor William Bligh, a retired ship captain, writes the following on the board:

- Power and influence
- Bigger is better
- Anger
- Emotional intelligence
- Bargaining
- Bullying
- Trading a chit for a chat
- Scorekeeping

Then he addresses the class: "Write a ten-page paper about how each of these concepts contributes to team conflict. I expect to see your papers in two days. Class dismissed."

Suggested Readings for This Exercise

- *Getting to Yes: Negotiating Agreement Without Giving In* by Roger Fisher, William L. Ury, and Bruce Patton
- *Crucial Confrontations: Tools for Talking About Broken Promises, Violated Expectations, and Bad Behavior* by Kerry Patterson, Joseph Grenny, Ron McMillan, and Al Switzler

Case 14.2

Jessica, Brianna, Ruth, and Zachary are assistant vice presidents in a large teaching hospital. Every month, they gather with their mentor, Dr. Lon Right, to talk about the challenges they face on the job and the trends in management and leadership. This month, they are discussing the book *Crucial Confrontations*.

Dr. Right: On the basis of our reading, what should be the ultimate goal in resolving conflict?

Jessica: To resolve the conflict and get compromise on the matter. Get the parties to meet halfway and then move on.

Brianna: I totally disagree. Compromising often means that you get poor results. Solving conflict does not mean you should give up on your key principles.

Zachary: I can see both sides. The real goal of conflict management, though, is to mount the debate but to do it in a respectful manner. Get the issue on the table, agree clearly on what the end goal is, and then hammer out the solution.

Ruth: In my view, practically all conflict is a classic power struggle. Human beings resolve these power struggles through fighting for their right to be heard. Compromises don't always happen, but what the book teaches us is how to negotiate with others so we don't damage the relationships we worked hard to build.

Questions

1. Is the ultimate goal of conflict management winning an argument, preserving a relationship, compromising on a solution, or all of these?
2. What lessons from this chapter and from *Crucial Confrontations* can be applied to your conflict management efforts?

Exercise 14.1

Read the vignette in the beginning of the chapter and answer the following questions:

- What kind of conflict is present in this situation? What are the short- and long-term effects of this conflict on the two nurse leaders involved, their chief executives, and the CNSs and nursing education?
- What should Jack's next step be?
- What organizational structure issues exist that gave rise to this conflict? How may they be resolved?

PART IV

EVALUATION

CHAPTER 15

Evaluating Team Values

THE MESSAGE OF this book is simple: The leader and the team (separately and together) must subscribe to a set of values that can support and enhance effectiveness and success now and in the future.

What are your team values? Does your team discuss these values? Are these values embedded in the norms and activities of the team? What team behavior and practice will you change or improve to live by these values?

Part III of this book explores the values that drive team functions and performance. This part is a guide for evaluating how well your leadership team (specifically its members) upholds those and other values.

KEY VALUES FOR ASSESSMENT

Team members should regularly evaluate the team's values. This activity reveals areas of deficiency and curtails harmful practices. The following list, along with the questions afterward, may be used to start a values discussion with the team. Team members may compare and contrast their answers and then offer suggestions for improvement.

Competence

Basic competencies are expected of every leadership team. (For an extended list of leadership competencies, see Dye and Garman [2006]). Specifically, team members must possess the triumvirate of skills—technical, decision making, and interpersonal. Each of these skills is critical for a leadership role, but together they strengthen the leader and make her a sustainable member of the team. The team member does not have to possess expert-level abilities, but she must be able to harness each skill at any time.

For example, if a team member has great technical acumen (e.g., finance, technology, business savvy) but lacks interpersonal skills, she may avoid opportunities to socialize with other members, display behaviors that alienate her staff and team members, fail to share or communicate information, and not participate in general discussions or team-building exercises. Similarly, if a team member has plenty of interpersonal charms but no decision-making instinct or technical abilities, he will not be able to perform the basic business responsibilities of a leader, let alone a team member.

Ask yourself: Does the team value competence? Do members of my team possess a triumvirate of skills, at least? If not, what improvements are needed?

Awareness

In an effective team, members are aware of each other's roles and responsibilities as well as the team's purpose, standards (or norms), and goals. Also, each member keeps abreast of current and future initiatives of the team. In this environment, all team members share information, discuss matters openly, and offer recommendations.

Ask yourself: Are all team members aware of our collective purpose, goals, and norms as well as each other's roles and responsibilities? If not, what improvements are needed?

Active Participation

Awareness comes from active participation in all that the team does, including meeting discussions, planning activities, goals and standards development, decision making, and role assignments. Even when not all members are directly involved or needed in a team activity, cooperative members are still considered participants because they attend meetings, volunteer their time and talent, express and listen to opinions and ideas, give feedback, contribute to the camaraderie, and support collaboration.

Participation is crucial in attaining buy-in. That is, if team members are involved in any team activity from the start, they tend to commit to the initiative and encourage others to follow suit.

Ask yourself: Do members of my team actively participate in our activities and initiatives? If not, what improvements are needed?

Cohesiveness

Team cohesiveness reduces personal animosity and organizational politics among members. It also increases the possibility that team goals will be achieved. Although cohesiveness presents several disadvantages, such as groupthink and low tolerance for change, it leads the way to cooperation and collaboration.

Ask yourself: Is my team cohesive? If so, is there an understanding among team members that cohesiveness, if not managed, could have negative consequences?

Commonality

A shared goal, values, or even a profession is sometimes enough to bond people together. If the commonality is a shared goal, the effort put into achieving that objective is maximized, as everyone is working toward the same vision. Having commonality also means that team members may require less explanation and convincing about an initiative and the ensuing process. One negative aspect of commonality is that it could lead to the formation of cliques, which harm the cohesiveness of the team.

Ask yourself: Does my team have a commonality? If so, how is it helpful? If not, what improvements are needed?

Commitment

When team members are committed (which is often brought about by cohesiveness and commonality), they work harder, set aside personal agendas, and contribute readily to the efforts. Simply, committed members are highly engaged; this level of engagement generates thoughtful questions, creative and multifaceted solutions, and ambitious but feasible objectives. More important, the undertaking to which the members are committed results in desired outcomes.

Ask yourself: Is my team committed to our purpose, goals, and tasks? If not, what improvements are needed?

Communication

Communication (including sharing of information and meeting discussions) enables the team to move forward. For work purposes, communication informs decision making, defines parameters (e.g., deadlines, goals, expectations, tasks), clarifies responsibilities, and prevents misunderstanding, to name a few functions. For interpersonal purposes, communication eases member interactions, assists with conflict resolution, and strengthens cohesiveness. Team communication—formal and informal, written and oral—should be regular, open, candid, and accurate.

Ask yourself: How well do my team members communicate with one another? Does our communication produce desired outcomes? If not, what improvements are needed?

Independence Versus Interdependence

Interdependence can be likened to cohesiveness in that it is good, but it has its limits. In other words, an interdependent team is naturally collaborative. The members are supportive of each other, and they can rely on each other to fill in gaps in skills, for example.

> The best team experiences occur when you can really feel the energy of the team. It feels synergistic. It's exciting.
>
> —Lisa Kimball and Amy Eunice (1999)

Too much interdependence can strip the individual members of their independence, which is dangerous in healthcare delivery. For example, an interdependent team usually makes decisions as a unit. If one member is unexpectedly gone, the rest of the team may not know what to do or may not be empowered to exercise their skills or authority. This indecision then is counterproductive and does not forward the team's function. This example works for both administrative and clinical teams.

Ask yourself: How interdependent is my team? To what extent do my team members rely on each other for support and input in decision making? Are team members independent or empowered to make decisions? If not, what improvement can be made?

Camaraderie

Camaraderie is the goodwill among team members. It is the basis of active participation, cohesiveness, and communication. Team camaraderie develops when members spend time outside of the work context to get to know each other. Although it can form between members who have nothing in common, camaraderie is strongest when a commonality exists (and sometimes, being a member of the same team is common ground enough).

Ask yourself: Is there camaraderie among my team members? What do we do to maintain it?

High Energy

High energy makes the team more productive, creative, and participative. Energetic members anticipate team meetings and do not view them as a chore. Also, they are eager to receive new assignments and tasks, their minds already computing the details before they even begin.

Ways to Boost Team Energy

• *Move a meeting to a different location, either each time or occasionally.* A change of venue refreshes team member interests because it connotes a new beginning. Many retreats are effective solely because they take place outside of the office.

• *Celebrate team and individual accomplishments.* Festivities reverse moods positively, and good moods hike up energy levels.

• *Invite guest presenters.* Trained presenters inspire and rally people to act.

• *Take a break from routine.* This break does not need to be work related, but it should be fun and meaningful. For example, team members could volunteer at a homeless shelter or food pantry.

Ask yourself: What is my team's energy level? Are my team members productive and eager? If not, what improvements are needed?

CONCLUSION

Every leadership team should periodically evaluate its values. If a team is productive and effective now (or "perfect"), imagine the even greater results it will achieve as it continues to lead by its values. Regular assessment of these values will help such a team sustain its success.

* * *

———————— **Self-Evaluation Question** ————————

* As a team member, what values do I espouse that may support or impede my team's function?

———————————————————————————————

SUGGESTED READINGS

Antai-Otong, D. 1997. "Team Building in a Health Care Setting." *American Journal of Nursing* 97 (7): 48.

Brown, M. S., J. Ohlinger, C. Rusk, P. Delmore, and P. Ittmann. 2003. "Implementing Potentially Better Practices for Multidisciplinary Team Building: Creating a Neonatal Intensive Care Unit Culture of Collaboration." *Pediatrics* 111 (4): 482.

Dunn, J. G., H. Holt, and N. L. Sport. 2004. "A Qualitative Investigation of a Personal-Disclosure Mutual-Sharing Team-Building Activity." *Psychologist* 18 (4): 363.

Goleman, D. 2002. *Primal Leadership: Realizing the Power of Emotional Intelligence.* Boston: Harvard Business School Press.

Huszczo, G. E. 1990. "Training for Team Building." *Training & Development Journal* 44 (2): 37.

Nursing Management. 1998. "Are First-Line Nurse Managers Prepared for Team Building?" *Nursing Management* 29 (10): 68.

Syantek, D. J., S. A. Goodman, L. L. Benz, and J. A. Gard. 1999. "The Relationship Between Organizational Characteristics and Team Building Success." *Journal of Business & Psychology* 14 (2): 265.

CHAPTER 16

Evaluating Team Effectiveness

How does your leadership team function? Is the team composition carefully put together, respectful of the organizational heirarchy? Are all team members involved in decision making? Are your meetings always, sometimes, or never necessary? Is the team bound to a set of protocols?

The team's structure (size, heirarchy, and membership) and primary activities (decision making, holding meetings, and establishing team protocols) greatly affect its effectiveness, just as team values do. This chapter presents the components that a leadership team should assess on a regular basis.

TEAM STRUCTURE

Size

As mentioned in Chapter 12, there is no ideal team size because every team has a different purpose, and this purpose dictates the number of members needed to make the team function well. However, there is such a thing as a team that is either too large or too small. Typically, a team that has 12 or more members is too large, while a team that has 4 or fewer members is too small. The problem with a large team is that decision making is slow, as too many people are involved in the process. With a small team, on the other hand, the expertise and experience of members may be limited, forcing the team to look outside for reinforcement and advice.

A team made up of 6 to 11 members works efficiently. Here, values (e.g., collaboration, cooperation) are more readily shared and learned, decisions are reached faster, tasks are more equally distributed, and conflicts are easier to spot and manage.

Ask yourself: Is my team too large or too small? When was the last time my team assessed its size? What are the advantages and disadvantages of resizing my team?

Hierarchy

Although humility is the virtue that prevents people from boasting about their accomplishments and even compels them to say "titles don't mean anything," it is not the same virtue that commands people to be truthful. The importance of titles and status within the organization cannot be minimized. They are important, especially to high-ranking leaders (the C-suite).

All the empowered, teamed-up, self-directed, incentivized [sic], accountable, reengineered, and reinvented people you can muster cannot compensate for a dysfunctional system. When the system is functioning well, these other things are just foofaraw. When the system is not functioning well, these things are still only empty, meaningless twaddle.

—Peter R. Scholtes (1998)

A leader's title is not merely a short description of her job responsibilities; it bears prestige and influence. As such, it should be given its proper place on the team's hierarchy. For example, an executive vice president should be ranked higher than an assistant vice president, and the two positions should not be given equal decision-making capabilities. One practice that fuels an imbalance of power among the team is granting undeserved titles either as an enticement for certain individuals to participate in an initiative or as a reward for an accomplishment that makes the team look good.

Ask yourself: Does my team recognize and respect the hierarchy among our members? Do we inappropriately bestow titles?

Membership

Membership on the leadership team is a coveted and highly esteemed post. Unfortunately, appointment to this team (or even an invitation to attend its meetings) is perceived by employees either as a privilege of being a leader or as a sign of cronyism. This perception is justifiable, given that some departments and interests have a disproportionately large representation on the team and at its meetings (see Exhibit 16.1 for examples).

To combat this perception, each membership appointment and invitation to meetings must be assessed according to practical, unbiased criteria, such as the following:

- The person's expertise, training, and skills
- The person's position and responsibilities
- The position's importance to the work and diversity of the team
- The position's potential contribution to the goals of the team
- Other work-related reasons for membership or attendance

Exhibit 16.1 Examples of an Imbalance of Power in a Leadership Team

- The public relations director is a member. She is in charge of disseminating organizational information to all staff.
- The senior vice president of patient care services and the vice president of nursing are members. Both have a nursing background and thus skew clinical discussions toward nursing issues.
- Although not vice presidents, the director of human resources and the chief information officer are members.
- The director of the medical staff regularly attends team meetings, but he is not a member.

TEAM ACTIVITIES

Decision Making

Many teams are proficient in delaying (not deliberately) decision making. Some teams discuss issues repeatedly but reach neither solution nor compromise. Other teams, meanwhile, are paralyzed by fear that any decision will create a conflict among team members. Yet decision making is a primary activity of a leadership team—an activity that cannot be delegated to another group or avoided without repercussions.

Often, the reason for this avoidance is the lack of a practical decision-making method. Specifically, basic components, such as the following, are missing:

- Facts and historical data about the issue at hand
- Brainstorming (for generating solutions and alternatives) and critical analysis (for examining ideas) tools and techniques
- Structured discussion method
- Well-defined goals and responsibilities
- Clear deadlines
- Trained leader or facilitator
- Participative members
- Time commitment

Meetings

Virtual meetings (which are more convenient) may eventually replace all traditional meetings, but even then team members will need to gather and discuss. And they should. Meetings, if well planned and well run, enable the team to think together, something that an e-mail or a phone call, although more immediate, cannot provide. In addition, meetings are a key contributor to building camaraderie. Meeting attendees almost always have an opportunity before and after the meeting to socialize with each other.

> In the typical senior working group, individual roles and responsibilities are the primary focal points for performance results. There is not incremental performance expectation beyond that provided by individual executives working within their formal areas of responsibility.
>
> —Jon R. Katzenbach and Douglas K. Smith (1993)

The backlash against meetings points to poor planning. That is, people greatly dislike meetings because (1) they are time wasters, (2) they do not ensure anything will get accomplished, (3) they are scheduled one after another (or there are too many), and (4) they are a platform for ad nauseum discussions and show-offs.

Poor planning is the root cause of these complaints. This section offers strategies that can improve the major components of a meeting.

Necessity

Unfortunately, meetings have been so ingrained in the workplace that only few attendees question their purpose and relevance. The rest of us just show up. This conditioning is costly because while the leader is sitting in an unproductive and haphazard meeting, revenue-generating opportunities could be passing her by.

Here are two simple ways to determine if your attendance is necessary:

1. Review the minutes or notes from the last meeting and the agenda (if available) for the upcoming meeting.
2. Ask.

Ask yourself: Are all of our team meetings necessary? Have I questioned their relevance?

Objectives, Agendas, and Handouts

Objectives specify the purpose of the meeting. If a meeting is called merely so that the team can share information or updates but no discussions are expected, team members may request to send in their information (via e-mail perhaps) and be excused from attending. Although this option is not available to everyone, such as the meeting chair, it can free up time for those whose absence from the meeting will not make a difference.

Objectives are typically found on the meeting agenda. An agenda lists the items to be discussed in order of importance or according to the meeting format. Equipped with an agenda, team members can minimize digressions.

Handouts (e.g., financial statements, statistical reports, proposals) distributed before the meeting help attendees prepare their comments, questions, or suggestions. Fortunately, the protocol at most meetings now is that any item that comes with a handout will not be discussed if the materials are not disseminated ahead of time. Without this protocol, much of the meeting time is wasted on explaining background information.

Ask yourself: Does my team distribute an agenda with clear objectives? Who determines the objectives? Do our meetings follow the agenda? Are our meetings structured so as to prevent side conversations, multiple discussions, and other interruptions? Do we require and distribute handouts or preparatory material?

Roles and Norms

As mentioned in Chapter 12, each team member must have a role to play (e.g., conscience, historian, devil's advocate). Such roles must conform to the norms (standards and expectations) of the team. For example, if the CEO is the "chair," he must come prepared, come on time, come to stay, come to listen, come to participate, and come to ensure order during the meeting.

Ask yourself: What is my role, and does it abide by the norms that my team has set? What are my team's norms, and do we follow them closely? Do cliques or factions exist within my team? If so, do they have a different set of norms?

Time

Meetings are ravenous eaters of time. Flexible meetings are wasteful because they encourage too much deliberation and too little resolution. Although thoughtful discussions prevent risky undertakings, they are impractical in an environment pressured by constant change and quick fixes. The biggest time wasters are information-sharing meetings, which must not last longer than three hours. Although meetings in which strategies are developed and shaped must not have time limits, they should still be scheduled in advance and planned. Part of this planning is distributing a summary or minutes of the past meeting to refresh attendees. The minutes are also a great tool for initiating discussion.

Ask yourself: How long do our meetings last? Do we have a regularly scheduled, time-limited meeting, or is it often flexible? Who keeps the minutes, and when are they distributed? Are the minutes detailed or vague, and are they useful for the next meeting?

Format

Generate creative ideas by making the meeting participatory. This interactive

---

Six-Point Team Effectiveness Evaluation

1. *Composition.* Are criteria followed in assembling the team? Who establishes and evaluates the criteria? How many members does the team have, and does this size benefit or disadvantage the team? Are major departments evenly represented on the team? How are members replaced when they leave? Does the team have subgroups to facilitate decision making and decisions, and if so, who assigns what members to serve on these subgroups?

2. *New-member integration.* How are new members integrated into the group? Do they go through a formal and informal orientation? When do the integration activities take place—before or after the member is introduced to the team? Who is responsible for ensuring that integration and orientation occur?

3. *Personality and style differences.* Is a structured tool—Myers-Briggs, Kiersey Bates, or Hogan Inventory—used to develop an understanding of different personalities and leadership styles? If not, how are these differences viewed and managed?

4. *Purpose, goals, and roles.* Who sets the purpose, goals, and roles for the team? Are all members involved in this process, and are these elements discussed by the team? Do all members have an understanding of each other's responsibilities and expectations?

(continued)

(continued)

5. *Protocols.* Are there rules and standards for decision making, interactions, behaviors, and other components of team function? Who established them, and are they well known to and practiced by the team? What consequences are levied against those who disobey the rules?

6. *Conflict management.* What methods does the team employ to manage conflict? Is the team aware of the areas in which conflict may be introduced (e.g., decision making, discussions, power structure)?

format enhances the team's awareness of others' responsibilities and expertise, and it also displays team members' personalities, which could help develop commonality and camaraderie. Following are common (and often visual) approaches used during interactive discussions:

- *Parking lot.* Innovative ideas not directly relevant to the current topic often emerge during a discussion. The parking lot is a way to save those ideas for later consideration.
- *Multivoting.* Multivoting is useful when the agenda lists too many items for discussion or consideration. Each team member is given a set number of votes to pick the issues (listed on a flipchart) she deems most important. All votes are cast confidentially to prevent political ramifications for the voters. The issues that receive the greatest number of votes remain on the agenda, and the rest are taken out. Multivoting is a democratic process that gives all members, especially the silent ones, a chance to be heard.
- *Affinity diagram.* This technique helps the team to organize and prioritize ideas and information. Using sticky notepads, team members jot down data or suggestions and affix them to a flipchart. These notes are then arranged according to themes or categories. For example, "use Twitter to create a buzz about the new 'green' maternity ward," could be grouped under "marketing and communication."
- *Process mapping.* Process mapping alerts the team to the intricacies (i.e., responsibilities, tasks, measures, objectives) of a specific workflow. This technique is helpful when modifying an existing process and when creating a new one.

Ask yourself: Are our meetings interactive and fun? If not, have we considered changing the format? What kind of participatory methods do we use?

Etiquette

Professional conduct must be expected in every professional setting. Distracting and rude behaviors (e.g., side conversations, flippant remarks) should not be tolerated during a meeting. Unfortunately, such behaviors, such as the following examples, can be observed in leadership team meetings.

> A leader is best when people barely know he exists, when his work is done, his aim fulfilled, they will say: we did it ourselves.
>
> **—Lao Tzu**

- Reading material unrelated to the team agenda to tune out an ongoing presentation (either oral or visual)
- Constantly stepping out to attend to a crisis or to take a break
- Constantly interrupting the facilitator or chair to ask a question, elucidate a point, complain, or argue
- Arriving late and unprepared
- Dominating the discussion and speaking out of turn
- Displaying dissent and impatience through body language, such as yawning, eye rolling, pounding on the table, and walking out
- Antagonizing a speaker or an idea with sarcastic comments and jokes
- Telling offensive (e.g., racist, sexist, elitist) jokes and anecdotes

The team, as a unit, should establish a code of conduct for meetings, post it in a visible setting or distribute it to all team members, and require all members to follow it. This code should include a clear statement about the consequences for not abiding by the rules. The team should also periodically discuss and evaluate the code.

Ask yourself: Has my team established etiquette guidelines? Generally, are my team members respectful? Typically, how does my team address inappropriate or distracting behaviors? What sanctions have been established for such cases?

Participation

Constant absence and nonparticipation may also fall under rude and distracting behavior. That is, a team member who is not actively engaged impedes or slows down the team's work. In addition, conflicts of interest may arise when only part of the team is involved and represented in the decision making.

The team could draw quiet members into the discussion by using various methods, one of which is the nominal group technique (NGT). NGT's process is as follows:

1. Identify the problem.
2. Ask all members to offer at least one solution.
3. Write down, on a flipchart, all the ideas as they are suggested.
4. Discuss, clarify, and evaluate every idea on the list. Eliminate those that are repetitive or not feasible.
5. Compile a final list of solutions as agreed on by the team.
6. Ask all members to vote on each solution on the basis of its significance to their priorities. Each member gets one vote.
7. Rank order the solutions according to the number of votes received.
8. Select the solution that garnered the number-one spot.

> **Ask yourself:** How engaged are my team members? Does my team encourage everyone to participate? What kind of tools does my team use to support an all-member discussion?

Wrap-Up

End the meeting right. Many meetings last so long that by the end, participants are so eager to leave that they fail to hear the last minutes of the discussion. The final minutes of any meeting should be the strongest because at this time the leader can rally support for the issues discussed and motivate the team to follow through. The team leader must conclude the meeting by providing a short—one or two sentences—summary of the issues discussed, the responsibilities assigned, and the steps that need to be taken by the next meeting.

Ask yourself: How does my team end our meetings? Do members leave exhausted and overwhelmed with too much information? How do we remind members of the decisions made and the next steps?

Protocol Development

All team members should be involved in developing the protocols that govern its behaviors, interactions, activities, decisions, and all other dealings. Equal participation by all members ensures that the protocols are not just created but also obeyed.

Following is an example of a decision-making protocol established by the entire team.

1. *Decisions must be made by all members, not just by a subset.* Because some teams are too large, their leader relies on a subgroup to deliberate on issues and make decisions. As a result, members outside of this subset may feel disrespected and could start a conflict. Conversely, members of the subgroup may feel arrogant and superior to the rest of the team. Although using a small group is a practical alternative to a lengthy all-member deliberation, it can harm team cohesiveness. If decisions must be made by a subset, the reasons must be explained to and discussed by the entire team. This way, everyone is aware of the intentions, and a rift is less likely to develop.
2. *A decision-making process must be determined for the issue on hand.* Will a vote be taken? If so, will the decision be determined by a majority? Do some members' votes weigh more than others? By discussing the process in depth, the team can avoid the Abilene paradox.[1]
3. *Divergent or nontraditional ideas must not be discouraged.* Unique perspectives can strengthen decision making, introducing innovative concepts or problems and consequences that the team may not have considered before.
4. *Team member expertise should not cause an imbalanced decision.*

Teams have the tendency to allow clinical decisions to be guided solely by the chief nursing officer or the chief medical officer. Members without such training can also offer meaningful and creative approaches.

5. *Proper decorum and courtesy must always be practiced.* Respect and honor in debate and deliberation are essential to effective team outcomes.

CONCLUSION

Inefficiencies can easily creep into the smallest details of a team. Regular monitoring and evaluation ensure that the structure and activities of the team still function in its favor. After all, an inefficient team cannot produce a successful outcome, let alone sustain it. See Appendix C for a team evaluation tool.

Note

1. One family made a long trip to Abilene, simply because one person suggested the location and the others believed that everyone agreed. As the family returned from Abilene, they discovered that none of them had wanted to go to Abilene in the first place.

* * *

—————————— **Self-Evaluation Questions** ——————————

* What is the composition of my team? Does the membership evenly represent the major areas in the organization?
* How are our team meetings conducted? Do we abide by certain rules of conduct during the meeting?
* What is our decision-making process? Are my team members involved in discussions?
* Has my team established team protocols? Do we follow these protocols?

CHAPTER 17

Self-Evaluation at All Career Stages

Tasha Rhona, a search consultant, and her close friend Rebecca Boling-Rodriguez are on the phone regarding a recent job disappointment.

Rebecca: Someone from the hospital just called to tell me I didn't get the CEO job. I have no idea why. I have the experience and the skills. My interviews went very well, or so I thought. In fact, two doctors approached me after the medical executive committee interview just to say they were looking forward to working with me. At the final interview, which felt like a welcome-to-the-club dinner meeting, the board chair and vice chair asked if I could think of any areas I needed special help or guidance with…

Tasha: How did you answer that?

Rebecca: With a no! What else am I supposed to say?!

Tasha: Let's calm down here. In your 20-plus-year career, this was the first time you competed in a job search, so how could you have really known how to prepare for an interview? I can't tell you why they passed on hiring you, but I can tell you what they might have been looking for. Are you ready to hear that?

Rebecca: I have a feeling you'll tell me anyway.

Tasha: When was the last time you did a self-evaluation of your skills, your style, your values—the whole nine yards?

Rebecca: Why? Is that important?

VALUES-DRIVEN LEADERS are self-assessors. They understand that they cannot expect others to speak, think, and act according to principles if they do not demand the same things of themselves. Thus, these leaders study their own moves and thought processes, with the dual intention of personal improvement and professional achievement.

All leaders—early, mid-, and late careerists—can benefit from evaluating their performance or practice in various areas related to their respective career stages.

ALL CAREERISTS

Personal Mission Statement

A personal mission statement is the road map of any careerist, preventing the person from veering off course and pointing to the desired destination ahead. This statement should answer the following questions:

- What is my purpose in life?
- What is my ultimate personal goal?
- What is my ultimate professional goal?
- What do I enjoy doing most?
- How and where do I make the most impact?
- How would I like my obituary to read? (Although morbid, this question forces you to think about your legacy.)

Writing this statement is daunting, taxing, frustrating, and awkward at first, but this tension eases after several drafts. Exhibit 17.1 provides examples of personal mission statements.

Reviewing the statement after a certain time is beneficial. Doing so will ensure that the document (1) is kept alive through daily deeds and words and (2) is revised to reflect the leader's values and goals. After several years, the statement can serve as a reminder of accomplishments and shortcomings. Some seasoned leaders have saved the mission statements they wrote when they were new to the field. One executive pulls out his old mission statements and self-evaluation notes annually. Revisiting them helps him find the "true north" of his personal life and career.

Ask yourself: Have I written a personal mission statement?

Exhibit 17.1 Sample Personal Mission Statements

Sample 1

My faith and my family are the most important things in my life. I want to be remembered by my family as a loving spouse and a caring parent. I want my children to remember that I did do an effective job of balancing work and home. I want my spouse to be comfortable with my desire to make a difference in healthcare.

I will end up compromising these values if I take a bigger, better job with more prestige. I do not want to do this. Therefore, I must be cautious in being tempted by these kinds of jobs. I will enjoy serving in an organization where I can make a personal impact without neglecting my children and spouse.

Although I want to be a CEO, I understand that the trade-off with my family is not worth that price. So, I will try to serve my CEO so effectively that he will include me in more of his decision making and give me greater authority, and I will gain greater fulfillment. This will give me much of the satisfaction typically enjoyed by CEOs.

(continued)

(*continued*)

I will try to work in organizations that respect and support work/family balance. I will try to show this same respect for my division managers.

At the end of my life, I would like to be remembered as a person who was effective in balancing both family and career and one who did not allow work and career to take over.

Sample 2

I entered healthcare to serve others. As a clinician, I studied the art and science of healing. I want to keep this healing mission the central focus of my working life. I want others to know me as a person who always puts patients first. I will be a good steward of the skills given me and will work to get others around me to develop and sustain the passion for patient care that I possess.

I want to work in organizations that put missions first and margin second. I do not want to be affiliated with organizations that are not committed to high quality. I do not want to work in the for-profit health sector.

Personal and Professional Style

The Kuder Career Assessment or the Myers-Briggs Type Indicators are among the most commonly used tools for assessing personal and professional style. Validated instruments are also available, such as the Hogan Personality Inventory; the Hogan Development Survey; and the Hogan Motives, Values, and Preferences Inventory. These inventory tools are applicable to the skills and styles expected of workers today, and they reflect the leadership competency systems that many organizations have begun to develop. Search consultant firms also employ assessment instruments to evaluate candidates.

Ask yourself: Am I aware of my personal and professional style? Do I use assessment tools, or do I rely on feedback alone?

Values

Constant review of values is imperative as they affect priorities, behaviors, mind-set, and performance. Team or executive retreats, performance reviews, self-reflection exercises, and mentor meetings are forums for thinking about and discussing these values.

Unfortunately, stories about senior executives who have committed unethical acts have dominated the news in recent years. Such incidents exemplify that (1) no one is immune to the seductive power of high office and (2) many careerists (from new to veteran) verbally support great values but do not understand how and why to live those values.

Especially in senior management levels—at which increases in revenues, market share, and physician and customer satisfaction rates are the primary focus—values-based concepts tend to be viewed as window dressing.

Personal values drive many professional values. In this way, a deficiency in one is a deficiency in another. For example, a careerist who values self-interest will tend to form or join a clique, sabotage cohesiveness and collaboration, and refrain from participating in initiatives that do not directly benefit him.

> This is the single most powerful investment we can ever make in life—investment in ourselves, in the only instrument we have with which to deal with life and to contribute. We are the instruments of our own performance, and to be effective, we need to recognize the importance of taking time regularly to sharpen the saw.
>
> —**Stephen R. Covey (1990)**

Ask yourself: What are my values? Are they aligned with those of my organization? If not, what is the difference, and is it hurting my chances of achieving my goals?

Continuing Education

Education should not stop with the completion of a graduate degree. In fact, such a degree is only an entrance ticket. Learning should be a lifelong pursuit because it makes the careerist more marketable, more in touch with current trends and practices, and more able to overcome challenges. Continuing education (both degree and nondegree programs) is offered by various entities, including professional associations, public agencies, private interests, and colleges and universities. Many such offerings are designed for working adults, as evidenced by the proliferation of webinars, distance learning, night and weekend classes, and accelerated programs. The most accessible and inexpensive forms of learning are reading industry-related publications and discussing trends with colleagues.

Ask yourself: How do I keep up with changes in the industry, in the management field, and in my role? What can I do to expand my knowledge and skill base? Is my organization supportive of continuing education? If not, what other avenues of learning may I explore?

EARLY CAREERISTS

Mentor Relationship

> Great organizations invariably decline. Great monuments eventually decay. Great accomplishments are always surpassed. All that is achieved invites its own eclipse. As long as life continues, there is more to be or do.
>
> —Lao Tzu

An early healthcare careerist undoubtedly has a lot to learn. Who better to serve as teacher than a practicing healthcare leader? Graduate health administration curriculum and professional management courses put much emphasis on the technical (including financial), administrative, and human resources aspects of leadership, but they often fail to cover behavior and ethics standards. A mentor can fill in for the new careerist the gaps that exist between education and practice, including interpersonal expectations. In addition, a mentor can link the new careerist with resources, provide advice and insight, clarify nuances, serve as a sounding board, and urge improvement.

Ask yourself: Do I have a mentor? What kind of relationship do I have with my mentor? Is this mentoring relationship beneficial to my career growth? If not, how may I improve it?

The Unexpected

Everything will be unexpected to the new careerist, especially in a fast-changing industry such as healthcare. Preparation is the best response to the unexpected. It makes the person think quickly and creatively, retain interest and focus, and be less intimidated by the unknown. For example, an early careerist is far less reluctant to try an untested, risky idea if she has done her research, spoken with experts and other experienced staff, weighed the pros and cons, designed a backup and response plan, and communicated the information she has with her direct reports. This way, if the idea develops an unexpected glitch later on, the glitch will not cause a major disturbance for those involved.

> **Ask yourself:** How well do I prepare for any activity? How do I respond to the unexpected?

Strengths and Weaknesses

An early careerist must be aware of his abilities and limitations as this knowledge puts him in control of what can be enhanced, what can be mastered, and what can be delegated (although this option only works for nonrequired responsibilities such as volunteering on a team). For example, if the person knows he is not good with numbers, he can attend budgeting and finance classes, ask others for help in understanding the concepts, and seek opportunities for practicing or applying the skill. Awareness of a personal limitation humbles a person, but it also serves as an impetus for improvement.

Early careerists can benefit from knowing what their leaders expect. One CEO distributes the following list of knowledge, skills, and abilities she demands from her team:

- Concise communication
- Focus on results

- Listening
- Strategic thinking
- Consistent and appropriate behavior
- Drive and initiative
- Persuasion
- Customer and team orientation

Ask yourself: What are my strengths and weaknesses? Am I committed to improving and mastering my skills? Do I understand the perils of my weaknesses?

Broad Perspective

Many early careerists tend to focus on only one organizational function—strategic planning, financial analysis, operations, human resources, or some other specialty. Although this practice enables the careerist to master a certain discipline, it curbs creativity and narrows perspective. During the first years, the early careerist should be a generalist, learning all the functions and their interrelationships. An early careerist is expected to ask questions and to listen intently. Everyone else feels obliged to share his or her knowledge and contribute to the early careerist's development. Nobody loses in this type of exchange.

Ask yourself: Do I shadow, ask, and forge relationships with people with diverse knowledge and specialties? How much do I know about the inner workings of my job and others' jobs? How may I widen my understanding and perspective?

Organizational Politics

Early careerists are primarily focused on gaining project experience. As such, they tend to be oblivious to the political undercurrents surrounding them. These power struggles are often common knowledge among staff, who suffer the consequences such as red tape, slow decision making, and multiple layers of approval. The early careerist should pay attention to signs of conflict and political upheaval, such as the following:

- Sudden departure of a well-liked, high-performing leader
- Distribution of multiple memos with divergent messages
- Side negotiations and secret campaigns
- Frequent "special" and "closed-door" meetings
- Increased backroom gossiping and theorizing
- Sudden cuts in budget, staff, and other resources
- Disruptions of routine
- Diminished morale
- Heirarchical or structural changes

Ask yourself: Am I aware of the political nuances in my organization? How do I find out about them?

Diligence

For an early careerist, every assignment is a test of skills, patience, persistence, and potential. Thus, the careerist must validate, double-check, corroborate, proof, and reference every piece of information, as any errors and omissions can be viewed as the result of sloppy work. This diligence helps the careerist develop great habits, which are the root of effective performance.

Ask yourself: Is my work meticulous? If not, what can I do to improve?

Job Opportunities

Some early careerists spend five to six years in their first jobs without considering (or experiencing) a promotion, a lateral move to a different department, or a position in another organization. Part of the reason may be loyalty and complacency, but more often than not the reason is fear. At this early stage, careerists should only fear stagnation and burnout, not the possibility of a job opportunity.

Staying in one place for a long time is admirable; in fact, many successful leaders retire from the same organizations that originally hired them. However, today's healthcare environment thrives on change and newness, demanding its leaders to follow suit.

One way to pursue change (and prevent burnout) is to apply for job opportunities. This process, including interviewing, enables the careerist to tout her strengths, assess her weaknesses, articulate her goals, discover her earning and career potentials, learn about the job market, and interact with professionals in another workplace. In addition, the process sharpens the careerist's communication and negotiation skills and presents a fresh perspective.

Ask yourself: How long ago did I apply for another job within and outside my organization? Am I confident enough of my knowledge, skills, and abilities to pursue a promotion, a lateral move, or a job opening in a different institution? Do I think the application process (even if I don't intend to leave my job) will be beneficial/harmful to my career growth, and why?

MID-CAREERISTS

Complementary Work and Home Life

"Busy" is the most succinct description of a mid-careerist's workday, which can stretch for more than 14 hours at times. These long days, not to mention occasional weekend events, wreak havoc on personal time and relationships.

The tug of war between personal and professional life is a stressor faced by most, if not all, mid-careerists. Although some are skilled at balancing these pursuits, many others struggle, leading to bad traits such as impatience, intolerance, arrogance, selfishness, and negative attitude.

Ask yourself: What can I do to live a balanced life? How is the imbalance in my life affecting my work, my relationships, and my future goals? To whom can I turn for help in this regard?

360-Degree Feedback

The 360-degree feedback instrument is the surest way to obtain frank comments from an array of people. The main reason for this is that the tool ensures confidentiality to participants, taking away the commenter's fear of reprisal. This, and other feedback tools like it, is helpful to the mid-careerist's development because the assessments come from those who work directly or have regular contact with the person. In addition, the tool evaluates a broad aspect of the careerist's performance.

Ask yourself: How often do I get feedback, and what tool do I use? Is the feedback I receive constructive or destructive? Do I promote the use of feedback to effect positive change? If not, why?

Networking

Networking breeds innovative ideas and fresh perspectives. It is most beneficial to mid-careerists because at this stage they have been in the field long enough to have repeatedly tried the same strategies but not long enough to have become cynical about novel approaches. In addition, networking gives mid-careerists another source for data and information, feedback, recommendations, and advice—all of which are essential to the work they do.

Ask yourself: What networking opportunities do I pursue? In what ways are they helpful?

Mentoring and Teaching Opportunities

Mentoring is beneficial to both parties involved. It allows the mentor to

- contribute to someone else's career development and growth;
- share insight about the implicit, unwritten, and unspoken rules of organizational life;
- offer advice on professional decisions that have the potential to turn into mistakes with long-lasting consequences;
- celebrate someone else's victories and provide counsel and comfort in that person's defeats;
- gain satisfaction and pride from being a vital resource, an advocate, a confidant, and a friend; and
- give back to (and do their part for) the healthcare community.

The questions that a protégé poses can also prompt the mentor to reevaluate her own career path or choices. For example, one former CEO admitted that she returned to being a chief operations officer after her protégé asked if she liked what she was doing. This question made the former CEO realize that she missed running day-to-day operations and the enjoyment she gained from that role.

Mentoring is fundamentally equal to teaching. Teaching, however, is structured, abides by rigid schedules, and requires much preparation. Practitioners are valuable additions to the faculty of any graduate program in health services administration because they strengthen the credibility of these programs. Many students prefer to learn from teachers who have field experience and who have applied (or created) methodologies explored in their textbooks and other course materials. More important, students gain much insight from teachers who have actually failed and succeeded at making real-world, organization-wide decisions.

Teaching provides ample rewards for mid-career practitioners, including the following:

> People are always blaming their circumstances for what they are. I don't believe in circumstances. The people who get on in this world are the people who get up and look for the circumstances they want, and if they can't find them make them.
>
> **—George Bernard Shaw**

- Opportunities to learn about (or at least become familiar with) new trends, forecasts, best practices, general and specific concerns, and public opinions—both within and outside the industry
- Opportunities for self-reflection, values reassessment, and career-choice reevaluation
- Forums for discussing healthcare-related news, history, customers, operational challenges, strategic approaches, and similar topics
- Regular lessons in humility, open-mindedness, diverse perspectives and expectations, relationships, and values

Both mentoring and teaching enhance the mid-careerist's performance levels, preparing him for his next role.

Ask yourself: Am I a mentor or a teacher? If so, what advantages does each role present? If not, have I considered mentoring and teaching opportunities? Do I have a mentor or teacher who has been part of my growth?

LATE CAREERISTS

Retirement Planning

For active and busy late careerists, thinking about retirement can be traumatic for several reasons. First, their level of control will diminish. Second, the pace of their every day will slow down. Third, the number of their associates will dwindle. Fourth, and most important, their sense of productivity and contribution will shrink.

Regardless of such trepidations, retirement is inevitable and thus must be faced accordingly.

The late careerist must develop clear plans (for home and work purposes) for her departure and communicate those plans with her family and staff. Financial preparation is imperative, but it is not the sole element of a robust retirement plan, which should include a next-career transition plan.

The plans of some retired CEOs include the following elements:

- A personal mission statement for the retirement years
- A phased plan for the next, less-rigorous occupation, such as being an instructor.

Note that retirement planning is markedly different from succession planning. The latter is a structured, multilevel development process, while the former is a personal transition exercise.

Ask yourself: How am I preparing—intellectually, financially, physically, socially, and emotionally—for my retirement? Are my family and staff aware of my plans?

Attitude Toward Younger Colleagues and Aspiring Leaders

Some late careerists question the values (including commitment) and contributions of "today's generation," regarding them with cynicism and skepticism. This negative attitude runs counter to the values espoused by the late careerist and harms team morale. It is also offensive to hear, even when said in jest. Seasoned leaders have accomplished too much to tarnish their reputation by making petty remarks.

Ask yourself: How do I regard the younger generation? Am I welcoming, or am I curmudgeonly? How do my colleagues respond to this attitude, and how are they affected?

Self-Tributes

Self-tributes are a documentation of not only the late careerist's achievements but also the positive changes to the organization, the community, and the lives of many people. Writing this tribute is not an exercise in egomania; rather, it is an exercise in self-affirmation—that is, your personal sacrifices eased others' hardships; you instituted improvements that saved lives and livelihood; your tireless advocacy and support led to progress in the community and the organization. After all, no one knows all the good that has been done better than the person who made it happen.

Ask yourself: What will people remember about me? Have I written a self-tribute? If not, what will I include in this document?

CONCLUSION

Finding time for self-assessment is easier said than done. But it is not impossible, especially when a strong commitment to improvement exists. Self-evaluation and self-reflection are routine practice for successful leaders because they understand that even the most ideal people can be "consistently inconsistent"—that is, everyone falls victim to saying one thing but doing another. If we are not aware of this tendency, we cannot begin to remedy it. This book offers not only a detailed explanation of this tendency but also a strong remedy.

＊　＊　＊
———————— **Self-Evaluation Questions** ————————

* Have I ever formally, using assessment tools, evaluated my leadership successes and failures?
* How well do I live by my values? Do I expect those around me to live by their values?
* What is my legacy?

CHAPTER 18

Maximizing Values-Based Leader Effectiveness

Jared D. Lock

THIS BOOK ASSERTS that leaders who understand, live within, and perform according to their values are personally and professionally successful. For the first edition of this book, the author asked me to write a chapter that linked this argument with strong empirical support. At the time, little was known about leadership in healthcare, and virtually no models of values effectiveness had been established. Today, ten years later, although healthcare executives are more aware of the connection between values and success, relevant literature in this area is still in short supply, and some studies (not empirical research) are poor in quality.

The reason I find some of these studies deficient is threefold. First, they were sponsored by private interests (e.g., assessment tool publishers, credentialing firms) to market their own products and thus are reductionist in nature; that is, they boil down this comprehensive concept of leadership to a short list of characteristics and offer no explanations about the drivers of success. Second, they are nothing more than personality surveys, which depend on subjective opinions and personal preferences rather than on evidence. Third, they present no unified or practical approach to understanding how a leader's values affect organizational success. As a result, such research fails to provide true measures of leadership values and effectiveness.

This chapter presents a framework—the whole-person evaluation model—for understanding leader effectiveness in the context of values. In addition, the chapter reviews findings from empirical research that support the clear connection between leadership values and high performance.

REVIEW OF THE LITERATURE

This section summarizes research findings regarding leadership performance—specifically, its outputs (effectiveness) and inputs (values and characteristics).

Defining Leader Effectiveness

Most healthcare organizations consider financial performance as the number one indicator of a leader's effectiveness. However, financial results do not identify what the leader did, why the leader did it, or what the leader could have done better.

Some studies define effectiveness as a *sustained* financial performance (e.g., more than 15 years), as compared with the competition. Organizations with sustained performance, the literature shows, have leaders who can influence the culture, impart their value systems on others, and get others to follow those values (Hogan and Blake 1996). Specifically, these leaders:

- Identify with and work in organizations that uphold the same goals and values as they do. With this kind of match, the leaders can easily motivate subordinates to perform according to their values (Borman and Motowidlo 1993; Guzzo and Shea 1992; Manz and Sims 1987).
- Control which goals are pursued in their organizations (Kouzes and Posner 2002).

- Change the value system (both positive and negative) of their organizations over time (Schneider 1987).

Research has also found the following:

- Leader values that are productive and in line with the organization's direction result in successful outcomes (Lock and Thomas 1998).
- Team counterproductivity is linked to a discrepancy between the leader's and the organization's value systems (Hackman 1987).

MEASURING LEADER PERFORMANCE: THE WHOLE-PERSON APPROACH

Research in this field has generated random and incomplete measures of leader performance. As an antidote to this haphazard approach, I have created a model (Exhibit 18.1) that evaluates and predicts performance using the components of a leader's persona and background.

Exhibit 18.1 The Whole-Person Evaluation Model

This whole-person model rests on the premise that a leader's performance is affected by the conditions surrounding the individual, not just by selected aspects. The model's five components (which tie to the concepts discussed in the book) are made up of the traits and conditions that research, conducted over the past decades, has indicated to be contributors to effective performance:

1. *Experiences.* This component includes skills, education, training, background, history, and other personal and professional achievements and experiences that influence the leader's work.
2. *Judgment.* This component describes the leader's cognitive process, including approaches to problem solving, decision making, and critical analysis. Judgment is the cross point between intelligence and personal style in that it comes from a person's intellect, values, and personality. This is why two smart people faced with the same problem will use different strategies and come up with different solutions.
3. *Values.* This component relates to a leader's fundamental beliefs and motivations. The values presented in this book are supported by the literature (e.g., Bentz 1990; Conger and Kanungo 1990; Hallam and Campbell 1992; Hogan and Lock 1995; Hogan and Hogan 1994; Lombardo, Ruderman, and McCauley 1988; Lorr, Youniss, and Stefic 1991).
4. *Positive Characteristics.* This component includes characteristics—such as initiative, diligence, and integrity—that facilitate the leader's ability to get along and get ahead in the workplace. Such traits enable a person to abide by his values (Hogan 1992; Kets de Vries and Miller 1986).
5. *Negative Characteristics.* This component contains qualities—mischief, dependence, and hostility—that derail or inhibit a leader's personal and professional pursuits. Typically, negative characteristics create a distance between a person and everything else, making her values difficult to share with and spread to others and causing low performance outcomes.

Each of the five components should be examined to determine how well or how poorly a leader will perform. Research by Carr & Associates indicates that the more of these components measured, the greater the accuracy of the prediction. More important, using a whole-person evaluation approach allows for a better diagnosis (and solution) of potential problems in leader performance.

> The field of leadership is presently in a state of ferment and confusion. Most of the theories are beset with conceptual weaknesses and lack strong empirical support....The confused state ... can be attributed in large part to the disparity of approaches, the narrow focus of most researchers, and the absence of broad theories to integrate findings from the different approaches.
>
> **—Gary Yukl and David Van Fleet (1992)**

VALUES AS THE KEYSTONE OF LEADER EFFECTIVENESS

Values, as illustrated in Exhibit 18.1, represent only 20 percent of a leader's whole persona. So, you may ask, why write an entire book that extols the virtues of values? The answer is simple: Research shows that a leader's effectiveness starts with and is sustained by her value system. Consider these findings:

- Leader effectiveness entails convincing others to put aside their own self-interests to work on common goals that will lead to positive outcomes (Lock 1997).
- A leader's personal value system is ingrained, was solidified early in life, and will continue to be a factor throughout his career (Dawis 1980).
- Leaders inherently look for organizations that share their values or that otherwise give them the best opportunity to live their values and stoke their motivations (Schneider 1987). For example, the value of helping others is supported and shared by a hospital that provides appropriate and high-quality care to anyone regardless of the person's ability to pay.
- The leader actively promotes organizational behaviors and activities that enhance his own value system (Lock 1996).

Leaders have a tendency (often unconscious) to be attentive to areas that serve their own interests but give mostly lip service to other areas that do not present opportunities for fulfilling their values. Subordinates watch their immediate leader (not the CEO or the mission statement) to see what areas the leader focuses on. The subordinates then mimic the leader's emphasis (Pollak and Weiner 1995). Given a leader's heavy influence on her direct reports, the leader's values must be in line with the organization's mission, vision, and values. Otherwise, counterproductive performance may ensue (Lock 1997).

- Employees stay with or leave an organization (or the immediate leader) on the basis of how well their focus or interests align with those of their leader (Doyle 1992). This alignment strengthens group identity and is thus beneficial to the organization, assuming that the shared focus (a) serves the organizational vision and goals and (b) leads to greater performance.

- Employee goal orientation is the most important contributor to how the team organizes itself and performs its organizational role (Hogan, Curphy, and Hogan 1994).

- Team effectiveness is directly related to the degree to which the team's and the organization's values and goals are similar (Meglino, Ravlin, and Adkins 1989).

In addition, research by Carr & Associates shows that values (which are distinct from personality and other traits) are the keystone to leader effectiveness. That is, values stabilize and strengthen performance, which in turn becomes a model for others to emulate.

The Link Between Human Needs and Values

Values are evolutionary in nature and stem from people's basic social needs—namely, to get along with others, to get ahead in our pursuits, and to create order in our lives (personal and professional).

Everyone has the same social needs, although the significance we give to each need varies, depending on our values. For example, corporate criminals, such as Bernie Madoff and Jeffrey Skilling, have a high need to get ahead but a low need to get along. Conversely, pacifists, such as Mother Theresa, have a high need to get along and low need to get ahead.

These social needs are automatic, ingrained, and largely unchanging. We create our own value system to enable us to meet our needs. For example, a leader will build trust (a *value*) to fulfill her *need* to create order in her organization. Exhibit 18.2 categorizes the values discussed in this book according to the three social needs.

Note that people's ability to make choices can cause the formation of *negative values*. Negative values are those that do not help us meet our basic social needs. For example, a leader who uses his position and power for personal gain idealizes self-interest and greed (negative values), which do not serve his needs for getting along, getting ahead, and creating order.

Exhibit 18.2 Three Social Needs That Underlie Values

To Get Along	To Get Ahead	To Create Order
• Respect	• Commitment	• Emotional intelligence
• Cooperation and sharing	• Ethics and integrity	• Cohesiveness and collaboration
• Conflict management	• Desire to make a change	• Trust
• Servant leadership		• Ethics and integrity
• Interpersonal connection		

The Link Between Values and Leadership

As suggested by the research cited earlier, a leader's values often mirror (and, over time, could eclipse) organizational values. Organizational values then reflect what the leader wants, how she wants to treat and be treated by others, and what activities and interests she would like to pursue.

Exhibit 18.3 provides a framework for understanding how the components of the whole-person model (see Exhibit 18.1) are affected by the leader's values.

1. *Experiences.* A leader's values regarding the experience component (e.g., lifelong learning, cross-training, workplace diversity) drive the initiatives pursued by the organization. When the organization changes its course (e.g., new boss, new vision) or no longer follows the values it shared with the

---

Exhibit 18.3 Values at the Core

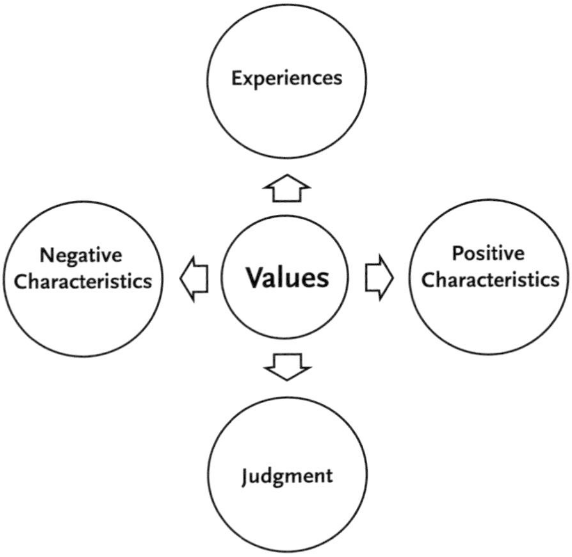

---

leader, the leader separates from the organization and finds another with which to share his experience values.

2. *Judgment.* This component—the leader's thought process—is values based. Although a leader's problem-solving and decision-making styles are grounded in personality characteristics, her analytical abilities are driven by her values and needs. In evaluating alternatives and outcomes, she will weigh which option or result best suits the organizational values. Positive or negative personality traits also play a role in the leader's decision making. The leader will use her judgment to assess the characteristics that get her closest to fulfilling her values.

3. *Positive and Negative Characteristics.* These two components live within everyone's value system. A leader develops characteristics to influence others to work in ways that enhance his values. Positive traits can facilitate this attempt, while negative traits may hinder it.

For example, a leader who values respect develops an ambitious and outgoing trait. He sets lofty goals for himself and others, and he socializes with those who are in positions of power. In the process, he comes across as arrogant and as a social climber. Judging by the negative reaction to him, this leader's attempt to fulfill his value is one-sided.

Research by Carr & Associates indicates that at least 50 percent of organizational leaders today display negative traits that cause stress, pressure, and poor performance among their employees. Although negative characteristics may deliver immediate results initially (e.g., bullies often get their way), they are not sustainable behaviors and are obstacles to achieving long-term values and needs.

Because positive and negative traits determine how well or poorly values and needs are met, successful leaders limit the negative and develop the positive. Having personal values that are in line with the organization's value system is great but is not enough;

the leader's traits must also be aligned with these values. The literature indicates that at least 80 percent of the development needs in the healthcare industry stem from a fundamental disconnect between professional values and personal characteristics. For example, many healthcare executives value servant leadership and work commitment and ethics. But the personal traits they develop—such as aggressiveness and blind determination—in pursuit of these values can alienate their followers and discourage them from giving honest feedback to these leaders. As such, the leaders are confounded; they do not understand why their direct reports are distant despite their efforts to be "servants" to their work, staff, and organization.

Competencies and Behavior

Competencies and behaviors, although not specifically addressed by the whole-person model, are nonetheless associated with this approach.

Behaviors tend to be more myopic than the model itself. They are a person's individual actions that, when reviewed in total by others, define that person's personal characteristics or traits; in other words, behaviors represent the *why* and the *how* of a leader's performance. For instance, hand wringing, hair flipping, and frowning are all behaviors associated with the characteristic or trait of anxiety. Competencies, on the other hand, are business-defined actions associated with several characteristics or traits represented across the model; in other words, competencies reflect *what* a person does on the job. For instance, when using the competency Strategic Orientation in the workplace, a leader will likely display characteristics associated with the Judgment component (e.g., intelligent, analytical), the Positive Characteristics component (e.g., open to new ideas, takes initiative), and perhaps the Negative Characteristics component (e.g., arrogant, easily distracted). The combination of these characteristics within a leader will lead to differential performance (as observed by others) on the competency.

SIX TENETS OF EVALUATING LEADER EFFECTIVENESS USING THE WHOLE-PERSON APPROACH

Assessing a leader's effectiveness is difficult in an environment overrun by thousands of performance measurement tools and theories. The following tenets—specific to the whole-person approach—are intended to help leaders accurately understand, diagnose, and improve their own and their team's performance.

- *Tenet 1.* Performance measures should be well supported by research and should focus on the specific factors that drive effectiveness in your organization. The evaluation instruments (see the appendixes) presented in this book can provide a start.
- *Tenet 2.* One tool for each of the five components of the whole-person model should be identified. Typically, this identification entails examining various instruments and methods.
- *Tenet 3.* Performance data on all five components should be compiled into a single, easy-to-understand report. This custom-content approach ensures that the data work to your advantage, not the other way around.
- *Tenet 4.* Assessments are the beginning of an improvement process, not the result. Accurate data and feedback force people to have direct, and even tough, conversations about their current inefficiencies. This discussion then leads to better outcomes.
- *Tenet 5.* Assessment should always go beyond the financial outcomes; it should include all five components of the whole-person model, including personal and organizational values. How and why the leader performs are just as important as the results she accomplished.

- *Tenet 6.* Measuring the Values and Negative Characteristics components takes creativity and diligence, given that the Judgment and Positive Characteristics components make up about 95 percent of all available assessment tools.

A PRACTICAL EXAMPLE FOR IMPLEMENTING THE WHOLE-PERSON APPROACH

This section is a step-by-step guide to applying to the workplace the concepts in this chapter and the values discussed in the book. The intent here is to show the clear connection between theory and practice; as such, this example could be used for teaching, discussion, and exercise purposes.

The work steps presented here are basic, but they will lead to a better understanding of leadership effectiveness. Organizations that want to maximize their leaders' values-based effectiveness will dig more deeply than this basic example allows, using well-validated measures of the five components of the whole-person model and creating detailed evaluations of leader performance.

Step 1: Define the corporate values. Most organizations have already completed this activity. If not, a quick survey of leaders is in order (e.g., ask, What are the top five values of our organization?). Typically, a healthcare organization has at least three common values:

1. *Excellence.* We are committed to achieving the best service quality and using only best-practice solutions.
2. *People.* We respect coworkers, patients, and others in our community and are committed to open communication and teamwork.
3. *Service.* We strive to exceed the expectations and standards of those we serve by consistently providing the highest quality care.

Step 2: Pair each corporate value to leader values. In many instances, corporate and leader values align. Here is an example using the values espoused in this book:

Corporate Values	Leader Values		
	To Get Along (social need)	To Get Ahead (social need)	To Create Order (social need)
Excellence	• Cooperation and sharing	• Commitment	• Ethics and integrity
People	• Respect in stewardship • Interpersonal connection		• Cohesiveness and collaboration • Trust
Service	• Servant leadership	• Desire to make a change	• Emotional intelligence

When matching corporate and leader values, the model will tend to show holes—that is, some leader values (categorized by social need) are not associated with corporate values; for example, in the table, the corporate value "People" is not associated with the leader value under "To Get Ahead." These gaps should be seen as an opportunity for discussion on how to better align corporate and leader values and why such holes exist.

If one of the identified leader values is not used with any of the corporate values, is that acceptable? Is it expected? Why is it not important for the organization? Does the organization need to change anything?

Practical Exercise 1: Using the grid (see page 235) as an example, fill out the People and Service corporate values based on your experiences.

Practical Exercise 2: Take your organization's values statement and complete the exercise for your organization. Where are the holes in your model? Are all of the leadership values used? Are some values used in almost all corporate values and others in just a few? Is that acceptable? Have this discussion with someone in your organization (or your classmates), and evaluate what you have learned and how well you completed the grid.

Step 3: Tie each leader value to the other four components (Experience, Judgment, Positive Characteristics, and Negative Characteristics) of the whole-person model. Use words that make sense to your organization, and provide specific characteristics instead of broad competencies. See the example grid.

Step 4: Tie each leader value to specific corporate effectiveness, competencies, and/or outcomes. Use words that make sense to your organization; it is more important to make the model easy to understand than to make it technically or scientifically accurate. For this step, ask the following questions for each component:

- *Experiences.* What organizational activities would a leader need to experience to test and validate the leader's willingness to follow this value?
- *Judgment.* If a leader shares this value, what would her decision-making style be? How would the leader solve problems? Would the leader focus more on data, processes, or people when making decisions?
- *Positive Characteristics.* What characteristics does a leader need to perform these activities? How would I describe a leader with this value? Think of a leader who lives by this value, and describe that leader. Place your answers in a grid like the example provided.
- *Negative Characteristics.* What characteristics would "deep six" a leader with respect to this value? If a leader is under stress and pressure, what poor characteristics would we see? Think of a leader who does not share each of the three corporate values (see Step 1), and describe that leader. Place your answers in a grid like the example provided.
- *Effectiveness, Outcomes, and/or Competencies.* We use these three labels interchangeably so as not to limit creativity. If a leader successfully lives by this value, what would the financial impact be to this part of the organization? How would it affect the people in the organization? How would it affect the patients? If the leader did not follow this value,

how would it negatively affect the organization? If a leader lived this value, how would others describe the leader?

Only one of the three corporate values (Excellence) is illustrated in the example grid below, which brings up a few points:

1. The example is broad, completed with one- and two-word explanations, and not inclusive of all associated information. Your own grid should be as detailed as possible to enable you to effectively see and understand your organization's and leaders' performance expectations and their impact on the organization.
2. The Experience component is not included in the example. However, note that a multitude of experiences can indicate value acceptance, and experiences tend to be defined after the fact—that is, when the leader needs to learn how to espouse the value in his work group.

Example Grid

Corporate Values	Leader Values	Positive Characteristics	Negative Characteristics	Judgment	Effectiveness/ Outcomes/ Competencies
Excellence	• Cooperation and sharing • Commitment Ethics and integrity	• Outgoing • Ambitious • Conscientious • Sensitive • Learning oriented • Persistent	• Distrustful • Selfish • Mischievous • Inconsistent	• Considers data as well as experiences • Evaluates plans for accuracy • Follows data results	• Continuously implements new processes as information is received • Ranks in the top 90 percent on all key customer-excellence ratings • Has high team ratings • Institutes zero-complaint goal
People	• Respect in stewardship • Interpersonal connection • Cohesiveness and collaboration • Trust	• ?	• ?	• ?	• ?
Service	• Servant leadership • Desire to make a change • Emotional intelligence	• ?	• ?	• ?	• ?

Step 5: Evaluate a leader's effectiveness following the example grid. It is best to start at the Effectiveness/Outcomes/Competencies side, starting with the far-right column first and then filling in the middle of the grid. The reason for this order is that most people are better at first identifying *what* performance or outcome they desire before determining *how* it should be accomplished.

Next, think about the leader being evaluated and highlight the effectiveness/outcomes/competencies, judgment, positive and negative characteristics, and values that this leader displays, and then leave the rest unhighlighted. This will then serve as the basis of a performance discussion. How does the leader stack up? Compare the highlighted and the unhighlighted items. What characteristics are not highlighted? Are these reasons the leader is not living up to expectations? Think of situations wherein the leader's deficiency (or presence of a negative characteristic) inhibited her from succeeding. What would you recommend to help the leader improve?

Step 6: Schedule a conversation with the leader. Explain the model, and discuss your findings with the leader. The leader should be actively involved in this conversation, offering comments, asking questions, and suggesting ideas for improvement.

Professional and Personal Values
Evaluation Form

OUR BEHAVIORS REVEAL our values more clearly than our words. Civility often prevents us from saying what we truly think, but it does not always prevent us from reacting with our body. As a result, we give out two varying reactions to one scenario.

This questionnaire assesses your values based on your perception and others' perception. It contains two tools—self-perception and others' perception.

Directions: After you complete the self-perception questionnaire, ask two to three fellow team members whom you think know you well to complete the Others' Perception questionnaire. Ideally a neutral third party should collect the completed questionnaires and compile averages and ranges for the answers. This might encourage others to be more honest when evaluating you. Following discussions with the neutral third party about the responses, you may meet with the individuals who evaluated you to compare and contrast all perceptions.

SELF-PERCEPTION OF VALUES

1. To what extent do you respect other people?

Not at All	To a Small Extent	Somewhat	To a Great Extent	Totally and Completely
0	3	5	7	10

2. To what extent do you serve as a good steward of the talent, authority, resources, and position you hold?

Not at All	To a Small Extent	Somewhat	To a Great Extent	Totally and Completely
0	3	5	7	10

3. To what extent are you an ethical person?

Not at All	To a Small Extent	Somewhat	To a Great Extent	Totally and Completely
0	3	5	7	10

4. To what extent do you keep your word?

Not at All	To a Small Extent	Somewhat	To a Great Extent	Totally and Completely
0	3	5	7	10

5. To what extent do you seek to develop positive and whole-some relationships with others?

Not at All	To a Small Extent	Somewhat	To a Great Extent	Totally and Completely
0	3	5	7	10

6. To what extent do you desire to serve others?

Not at All	To a Small Extent	Somewhat	To a Great Extent	Totally and Completely
0	3	5	7	10

7. To what extent do you desire to make a difference and effect positive changes and contributions?

Not at All	To a Small Extent	Somewhat	To a Great Extent	Totally and Completely
0	3	5	7	10

8. To what extent are you committed to the vision and goals of your organization?

Not at All	To a Small Extent	Somewhat	To a Great Extent	Totally and Completely
0	3	5	7	10

9. To what extent do you work hard?

Not at All	To a Small Extent	Somewhat	To a Great Extent	Totally and Completely
0	3	5	7	10

10. To what extent are you a highly dedicated person?

Not at All	To a Small Extent	Somewhat	To a Great Extent	Totally and Completely
0	3	5	7	10

11. To what extent are you emotionally mature?

Not at All	To a Small Extent	Somewhat	To a Great Extent	Totally and Completely
0	3	5	7	10

12. To what extent do you value the contributions of a team?

Not at All	To a Small Extent	Somewhat	To a Great Extent	Totally and Completely
0	3	5	7	10

13. To what extent do you cooperate with fellow team members?

Not at All	To a Small Extent	Somewhat	To a Great Extent	Totally and Completely
0	3	5	7	10

14. To what extent do you share information and other resources with fellow team members?

Not at All	To a Small Extent	Somewhat	To a Great Extent	Totally and Completely
0	3	5	7	10

15. To what extent do you try to build trust with others?

Not at All	To a Small Extent	Somewhat	To a Great Extent	Totally and Completely
0	3	5	7	10

16. To what extent are you willing to trust others?

Not at All	To a Small Extent	Somewhat	To a Great Extent	Totally and Completely
0	3	5	7	10

17. To what extent do you affirmatively try to bring conflict to the surface to manage it effectively?

Not at All	To a Small Extent	Somewhat	To a Great Extent	Totally and Completely
0	3	5	7	10

OTHERS' PERCEPTION OF_____ VALUES
(insert name here)

1. To what extent does your colleague respect other people?

Not at All	To a Small Extent	Somewhat	To a Great Extent	Totally and Completely
0	3	5	7	10

2. To what extent does your colleague serve as a good steward of the talent, authority, resources, and position she/he holds?

Not at All	To a Small Extent	Somewhat	To a Great Extent	Totally and Completely
0	3	5	7	10

3. To what extent is your colleague an ethical person?

Not at All	To a Small Extent	Somewhat	To a Great Extent	Totally and Completely
0	3	5	7	10

4. To what extent can your colleague keep her/his word?

Not at All	To a Small Extent	Somewhat	To a Great Extent	Totally and Completely
0	3	5	7	10

5. To what extent does your colleague seek to develop positive and wholesome relationships with others?

Not at All	To a Small Extent	Somewhat	To a Great Extent	Totally and Completely
0	3	5	7	10

6. To what extent does your colleague desire to serve others?

Not at All	To a Small Extent	Somewhat	To a Great Extent	Totally and Completely
0	3	5	7	10

7. To what extent does your colleague desire to make a difference and effect positive changes and contributions?

Not at All	To a Small Extent	Somewhat	To a Great Extent	Totally and Completely
0	3	5	7	10

8. To what extent is your colleague committed to the vision and goals of your organization?

Not at All	To a Small Extent	Somewhat	To a Great Extent	Totally and Completely
0	3	5	7	10

9. To what extent does your colleague work hard?

Not at All	To a Small Extent	Somewhat	To a Great Extent	Totally and Completely
0	3	5	7	10

10. To what extent is your colleague a highly dedicated person?

Not at All	To a Small Extent	Somewhat	To a Great Extent	Totally and Completely
0	3	5	7	10

11. To what extent is your colleague emotionally mature?

Not at All	To a Small Extent	Somewhat	To a Great Extent	Totally and Completely
0	3	5	7	10

12. To what extent does your colleague value the contributions of a team?

Not at All	To a Small Extent	Somewhat	To a Great Extent	Totally and Completely
0	3	5	7	10

13. To what extent does your colleague cooperate with fellow team members?

Not at All	To a Small Extent	Somewhat	To a Great Extent	Totally and Completely
0	3	5	7	10

14. To what extent does your colleague share information and other resources with fellow team members?

Not at All	To a Small Extent	Somewhat	To a Great Extent	Totally and Completely
0	3	5	7	10

15. To what extent does your colleague try to build trust with others?

Not at All	To a Small Extent	Somewhat	To a Great Extent	Totally and Completely
0	3	5	7	10

16. To what extent is your colleague willing to trust others?

Not at All	To a Small Extent	Somewhat	To a Great Extent	Totally and Completely
0	3	5	7	10

17. To what extent does your colleague affirmatively try to bring conflict to the surface to manage it effectively?

Not at All	To a Small Extent	Somewhat	To a Great Extent	Totally and Completely
0	3	5	7	10

Emotional Intelligence
Evaluation Form

EMOTIONAL INTELLIGENCE IS a person's maturity quotient. Maturity is the ability to manage emotions, make sound decisions, positively influence others, and be self-aware. The questions in this instrument assess the emotional intelligence of a person in the workplace based on the perception of those she/he works, or worked, directly with.

Directions: Read each question carefully and circle the answer that most appropriately describes the person being evaluated. There are no right or wrong answers, but carefully reflect on each question and answer.

You have been asked to evaluate _____ along several interpersonal dimensions. Five or more individuals—peers and subordinates—are completing this questionnaire. When you are finished, please return your questionnaire to ___(name of third party)___, who will compile the results and provide summary averages to the person named above. Because the questionnaire does not require your name, your participation is anonymous; please do not share your responses with anyone.

What is your relationship to the person being evaluated? Please check one.

_____ Peer (work at same organization)

_____ Peer (work elsewhere)

_____ Subordinate

_____ Superior (full-time paid boss)

_____ Superior (voluntary board member)

_____ Other

1. This leader creates the feeling that she/he looks forward to each day with positive anticipation.

Strongly Disagree	Disagree	Neither Disagree or Agree	Agree	Strongly Agree
1	2	3	4	5

2. This leader truly believes that her/his work really makes a difference in her/his organization.

Strongly Disagree	Disagree	Neither Disagree or Agree	Agree	Strongly Agree
1	2	3	4	5

3. This leader has an even temper.

Strongly Disagree	Disagree	Neither Disagree or Agree	Agree	Strongly Agree
1	2	3	4	5

4. This leader rarely gets frustrated.

Strongly Disagree	Disagree	Neither Disagree or Agree	Agree	Strongly Agree
1	2	3	4	5

5. This leader has the creative ability to solve problems among people.

Strongly Disagree	Disagree	Neither Disagree or Agree	Agree	Strongly Agree
1	2	3	4	5

6. This leader truly enjoys being with other people.

Strongly Disagree	Disagree	Neither Disagree or Agree	Agree	Strongly Agree
1	2	3	4	5

7. This leader has strong control over her/his emotions.

Strongly Disagree	Disagree	Neither Disagree or Agree	Agree	Strongly Agree
1	2	3	4	5

8. When times get tough in the work setting, others can turn to this leader for guidance.

Strongly Disagree	Disagree	Neither Disagree or Agree	Agree	Strongly Agree
1	2	3	4	5

9. When mistakes are made, this leader's first instinct is to take corrective action (rather than place blame).

Strongly Disagree	Disagree	Neither Disagree or Agree	Agree	Strongly Agree
1	2	3	4	5

10. Other people would describe this leader as a person who does not "fall apart" under pressure.

Strongly Disagree	Disagree	Neither Disagree or Agree	Agree	Strongly Agree
1	2	3	4	5

11. This leader is well suited for her/his career.

Strongly Disagree	Disagree	Neither Disagree or Agree	Agree	Strongly Agree
1	2	3	4	5

12. If this leader had the chance to start her/his career all over again, she/he would still choose a leadership position.

Strongly Disagree	Disagree	Neither Disagree or Agree	Agree	Strongly Agree
1	2	3	4	5

13. This leader respects other people.

Strongly Disagree	Disagree	Neither Disagree or Agree	Agree	Strongly Agree
1	2	3	4	5

14. This leader is highly motivated.

Strongly Disagree	Disagree	Neither Disagree or Agree	Agree	Strongly Agree
1	2	3	4	5

15. Others would say this leader has her/his ego under control.

Strongly Disagree	Disagree	Neither Disagree or Agree	Agree	Strongly Agree
1	2	3	4	5

16. This leader has an appropriately high level of self-esteem.

Strongly Disagree	Disagree	Neither Disagree or Agree	Agree	Strongly Agree
1	2	3	4	5

17. Although this leader may at times get upset or angry, she/he has the ability to control emotions.

Strongly Disagree	Disagree	Neither Disagree or Agree	Agree	Strongly Agree
1	2	3	4	5

18. This leader has an appropriately high level of motivation.

Strongly Disagree	Disagree	Neither Disagree or Agree	Agree	Strongly Agree
1	2	3	4	5

19. This leader always seeks win–win solutions in conflict situations.

Strongly Disagree	Disagree	Neither Disagree or Agree	Agree	Strongly Agree
1	2	3	4	5

20. This leader would be the last person I would describe as a hopeless individual.

Strongly Disagree	Disagree	Neither Disagree or Agree	Agree	Strongly Agree
1	2	3	4	5

21. Although impatient for positive results, this leader does not allow her/his impatience to create a negative working environment.

Strongly Disagree	Disagree	Neither Disagree or Agree	Agree	Strongly Agree
1	2	3	4	5

22. This leader is a person whom others trust.

Strongly Disagree	Disagree	Neither Disagree or Agree	Agree	Strongly Agree
1	2	3	4	5

23. This leader is appropriately self-confident without being overbearing.

Strongly Disagree	Disagree	Neither Disagree or Agree	Agree	Strongly Agree
1	2	3	4	5

24. This leader is sensitive to others' feelings.

Strongly Disagree	Disagree	Neither Disagree or Agree	Agree	Strongly Agree
1	2	3	4	5

25. This leader listens well.

Strongly Disagree	Disagree	Neither Disagree or Agree	Agree	Strongly Agree
1	2	3	4	5

26. The last description you would expect to hear of this leader is "flies off the handle a lot."

Strongly Disagree	Disagree	Neither Disagree or Agree	Agree	Strongly Agree
1	2	3	4	5

27. This leader maintains a good balance in life.

Strongly Disagree	Disagree	Neither Disagree or Agree	Agree	Strongly Agree
1	2	3	4	5

28. This leader is emotionally stable and healthy.

Strongly Disagree	Disagree	Neither Disagree or Agree	Agree	Strongly Agree
1	2	3	4	5

29. This leader faces setbacks and adversity well.

Strongly Disagree	Disagree	Neither Disagree or Agree	Agree	Strongly Agree
1	2	3	4	5

30. This leader would not be described as hostile.

Strongly Disagree	Disagree	Neither Disagree or Agree	Agree	Strongly Agree
1	2	3	4	5

31. This leader has developed good mechanisms to get feedback from others.

Strongly Disagree	Disagree	Neither Disagree or Agree	Agree	Strongly Agree
1	2	3	4	5

Leadership Team Evaluation Form

ALTHOUGH THIS QUESTIONNAIRE has not been validated (i.e., no study has been performed to determine the correlation between the results of this questionnaire and performance outcome—such as profitability, patient satisfaction, physician satisfaction, and employee satisfaction), it provides the team an initial tool for assessing the components of team effectiveness.

Because each component contributes to the overall efficiencies and inefficiencies of the team, each must be independently evaluated. To ensure comprehensive representation, all team members must complete the questionnaire. To ensure confidentiality of the responses, the team must select a neutral third party to collect the questionnaires, tally the ratings, and write a report, which will be distributed to the team for discussion.

Directions: Rate the following questions as correctly as possible. Please submit your completed questionnaire to _____(name of third party)_____ by __(date)__ . Please do not share your responses with others.

TEAM LEADERSHIP

1. The CEO or leader is not autocratic.

Strongly Disagree	Disagree	Neither Disagree or Agree	Agree	Strongly Agree
1	2	3	4	5

2. The CEO or leader does not make team decisions outside meetings. The CEO or leader develops an atmosphere that encourages openness.

Strongly Disagree	Disagree	Neither Disagree or Agree	Agree	Strongly Agree
1	2	3	4	5

3. The CEO or leader is not afraid to be a full and equal participant in team processes.

Strongly Disagree	Disagree	Neither Disagree or Agree	Agree	Strongly Agree
1	2	3	4	5

4. In establishing the team, the CEO or leader ensures that all team members understand the decisions that should

be made within the team setting and the decisions that
should be made outside the team setting.

Strongly Disagree	Disagree	Neither Disagree or Agree	Agree	Strongly Agree
1	2	3	4	5

5. The CEO or leader ensures that time is set aside to
    occasionally discuss roles and decision-making rules and
    protocols.

Strongly Disagree	Disagree	Neither Disagree or Agree	Agree	Strongly Agree
1	2	3	4	5

TEAM COMPATIBILITY

6. Members share common values and goals.

Strongly Disagree	Disagree	Neither Disagree or Agree	Agree	Strongly Agree
1	2	3	4	5

7.   Members have personal compatibility.

Strongly Disagree	Disagree	Neither Disagree or Agree	Agree	Strongly Agree
1	2	3	4	5

8.   Members have professional compatibility.

Strongly Disagree	Disagree	Neither Disagree or Agree	Agree	Strongly Agree
1	2	3	4	5

TEAM INTERACTION

9.   Members have camaraderie.

Strongly Disagree	Disagree	Neither Disagree or Agree	Agree	Strongly Agree
1	2	3	4	5

10. Members occasionally socialize outside of the workplace.

Strongly Disagree	Disagree	Neither Disagree or Agree	Agree	Strongly Agree
1	2	3	4	5

11. The team has frequent communication.

Strongly Disagree	Disagree	Neither Disagree or Agree	Agree	Strongly Agree
1	2	3	4	5

12. The team has open and candid conversations.

Strongly Disagree	Disagree	Neither Disagree or Agree	Agree	Strongly Agree
1	2	3	4	5

13. The team exchanges accurate and timely information, prohibits or limits exaggeration, and discourages information hiding.

Strongly Disagree	Disagree	Neither Disagree or Agree	Agree	Strongly Agree
1	2	3	4	5

TEAM MIND-SET AND STRUCTURE

14. Members are committed to the same goals.

Strongly Disagree	Disagree	Neither Disagree or Agree	Agree	Strongly Agree
1	2	3	4	5

15. Each member understands her/his role within the team.

Strongly Disagree	Disagree	Neither Disagree or Agree	Agree	Strongly Agree
1	2	3	4	5

16. Members have actively and openly discussed team roles.

Strongly Disagree	Disagree	Neither Disagree or Agree	Agree	Strongly Agree
1	2	3	4	5

17. Members have mutually agreed to the assignment of team roles.

Strongly Disagree	Disagree	Neither Disagree or Agree	Agree	Strongly Agree
1	2	3	4	5

18. Members are highly interdependent with one another.

Strongly Disagree	Disagree	Neither Disagree or Agree	Agree	Strongly Agree
1	2	3	4	5

19. The team has a high energy level.

Strongly Disagree	Disagree	Neither Disagree or Agree	Agree	Strongly Agree
1	2	3	4	5

20. Conflict is acknowledged, discussed, and managed by all members.

Strongly Disagree	Disagree	Neither Disagree or Agree	Agree	Strongly Agree
1	2	3	4	5

21. Members are frank with each other and engage in little politics.

Strongly Disagree	Disagree	Neither Disagree or Agree	Agree	Strongly Agree
1	2	3	4	5

22. The size of the team is between 6 and 11.

Strongly Disagree	Disagree	Neither Disagree or Agree	Agree	Strongly Agree
1	2	3	4	5

23. There is a proper balance of titles among members.

Strongly Disagree	Disagree	Neither Disagree or Agree	Agree	Strongly Agree
1	2	3	4	5

TEAM MEETINGS

24. Meetings are well organized.

Strongly Disagree	Disagree	Neither Disagree or Agree	Agree	Strongly Agree
1	2	3	4	5

25. Meetings have objectives.

Strongly Disagree	Disagree	Neither Disagree or Agree	Agree	Strongly Agree
1	2	3	4	5

26. The agenda is followed closely during meetings.

Strongly Disagree	Disagree	Neither Disagree or Agree	Agree	Strongly Agree
1	2	3	4	5

27. Members show appropriate courtesy to each other during meetings.

Strongly Disagree	Disagree	Neither Disagree or Agree	Agree	Strongly Agree
1	2	3	4	5

28. All members actively participate in meetings.

Strongly Disagree	Disagree	Neither Disagree or Agree	Agree	Strongly Agree
1	2	3	4	5

29. Meetings have an appropriate level of formality but are not stiff.

Strongly Disagree	Disagree	Neither Disagree or Agree	Agree	Strongly Agree
1	2	3	4	5

30. Meetings are ended with an understood conclusion.

Strongly Disagree	Disagree	Neither Disagree or Agree	Agree	Strongly Agree
1	2	3	4	5

TEAM DECISIONS

31. The team observes decision-making protocols.

Strongly Disagree	Disagree	Neither Disagree or Agree	Agree	Strongly Agree
1	2	3	4	5

32. The entire team is responsible for decision making.

Strongly Disagree	Disagree	Neither Disagree or Agree	Agree	Strongly Agree
1	2	3	4	5

33. The entire team has been trained in decision-making techniques.

Strongly Disagree	Disagree	Neither Disagree or Agree	Agree	Strongly Agree
1	2	3	4	5

34. The team has openly discussed its decision-making styles and processes.

Strongly Disagree	Disagree	Neither Disagree or Agree	Agree	Strongly Agree
1	2	3	4	5

35. The entire team realizes the danger of using compromise as the only end result of a decision-making process.

Strongly Disagree	Disagree	Neither Disagree or Agree	Agree	Strongly Agree
1	2	3	4	5

References

Adams, S. 1996. *The Dilbert Principle: A Cubicle's-Eye View of Bosses, Meetings, Management Fads and Other Workplace Afflictions.* New York: HarperBusiness.

Band, W. A. 1994. "Touchstones: Ten New Ideas Revolutionizing Business." In *Organizational Behavior,* 4th edition, edited by R. Kreitner and A. Kinicki. New York: Richard D. Irwin.

Bennis, W., and R. Townsend. 1997. *Reinventing Leadership: Strategies to Empower the Organization.* New York: William Morrow and Co.

Benton, D. A. 1992. *Lions Don't Need to Roar: Using the Leadership Power of Professional Presence to Stand Out, Fit in and Move Ahead.* New York: Warner Books.

Bentz, J. 1990. "Contextual Issues in Predicting High-Level Leadership Performance." In *Measures of Leadership,* edited by K. Clark and M. Clark, 131–43. West Orange, NJ: Leadership Library of America.

Berlin. L. 2006. "Will Saying 'I'm Sorry' Prevent a Malpractice Lawsuit?" *Americal Journal of Roentgenology* 187: 10–15.

Berthold, J. 2008. "Is the Generation Gap a Growth Opportunity?" *ACP Internist.* [Online article; retrieved 11/23/09.] www.acpinternist.org/archives/2008/04/two.htm.

BizTimes. 2009. "The Servant Leader: Richard Pieper, Sr."
[Online information; retrieved 12/1/09.] www.biztimes.com/
news/2009/2/20/the-servant-leaderrichard-pieper-sr.

Block, P. 1993. *Stewardship: Choosing Service Over Self-Interest.*
San Francisco: Berrett-Koehler Publishers.

Borman, W., and S. Motowidlo. 1993. "Expanding the Criterion
Domain." In *Personnel Selection in Organizations,* edited by
N. Schmitt, W. Borman, and Associates. San Francisco:
Jossey-Bass Publishers.

Branden, N. 1998. "The Psychology of Self-Esteem." In *Heart at
Work,* edited by J. Canfield and J. Miller. New York:
McGraw-Hill.

Bricker & Eckler. 2009. "The Joint Commission Implements
New Conflict Management Standard." [Online information;
retrieved 12/13/09.] www.bricker.com/documents/
publications/1844.pdf

Burns, J. M. 1978. *Leadership.* New York: Harper and Row.

Collins, J. 2001. *Good to Great: Why Some Companies Make the
Leap... and Others Don't.* New York: HarperCollins.

Conger, J. 1989. *The Charismatic Leader: Behind the Mystic of
Exceptional Leadership.* San Francisco: Jossey-Bass Publishers.

Conger, J., and R. Kanungo. 1990. "A Behavioral Attribute
Measure." Paper presented at the annual meeting of the
Academy of Management, San Francisco.

Cooper, R. K., and A. Sawaf. 1997. *Executive EQ: Emotional
Intelligence in Leadership and Organizations.* New York:
Perigee Books, The Berkley Publishing Co.

Covey, S. R. 1990. *The Seven Habits of Highly Effective People:
Powerful Lessons in Personal Change.* New York: Fireside Press.

————. 1992. *Principle-Centered Leadership.* New York: Fireside
Press.

Covey, S. M. R. 2008. *The Speed of Trust: The One Thing That
Changes Everything.* New York: Free Press.

Dawis, R. V. 1980. "Measuring Interests." *New Directions in
Testing and Measurement* 7: 77–91.

Doyle. 1992. "Caution: Self-Directed Work Teams." *HR Magazine* (June): 153–54.

Dye, C. 2000. *Executive Excellence.* Chicago: Health Administration Press.

Dye, C. F., and A. N. Garman. 2006. *Exceptional Leadership: 16 Critical Competencies for Healthcare Leaders.* Chicago: Health Administration Press.

Drucker, P. 1997. "Getting Beyond Industrial Logic: Renewing Our Faith in the Value of Health," by Shari Mycek. *Healthcare Forum Journal* 40 (4): 16–20.

Eisenhardt, K. M., J. L. Kahwajy, and L. J. Bourgeois, III. 1997. "How Management Teams Can Have a Good Fight." *Harvard Business Review* (July–August): 77.

Engstrom, T. W., and E. R. Dayton. 1984. *The Christian Leader's 60-Second Management Guide.* Waco, TX: Word Books.

Fulghum, R. 1993. *All I Really Need to Know I Learned in Kindergarten: Uncommon Thoughts on Common Things.* New York: Ballantine Books.

Gallup. 2009a. "Driving Engagement by Focusing on Strengths." [Online article; retrieved 11/23/09.] http://gmj.gallup.com/home.

———. 2009b. "Employee Engagement." [Online information; retrieved 12/1/09.] www.gallup.com/consulting/healthcare/15382/employee-engagement.aspx.

Garber, P. 2004. *Giving and Receiving Performance Feedback.* Amherst, MA: HRD Press, Inc.

Garman, A. N., and C. F. Dye. 2009. *The Healthcare C-Suite: Leadership Development at the Top.* Chicago: Health Administration Press.

Garman, A., and J. L. Tyler. 2007. *Succession Planning Practices & Outcomes in U.S. Hospital Systems: Final Report.* Chicago: American College of Healthcare Executives.

George, B. 2003. *Authentic Leadership: Rediscovering the Secrets to Creating Lasting Value.* San Francisco: Jossey-Bass.

Goldsmith, J. 1998. "Three Predictable Crises in the Health

System and What to Do About Them." *Healthcare Forum Journal* (November–December).

Goleman, D. 1998. *Working with Emotional Intelligence.* New York: Bantam Books.

Greenleaf, R. K. 1983. *Servant Leadership: A Journey into the Nature of Legitimate Power and Greatness.* Mahwah, NJ: The Paulist Press.

———. 2009. "What Is Servant Leadership?" [Online information; retrieved 12/1/09.] www.greenleaf.org.

Guzzo, R., and G. Shea. 1992. "Group Performance and Intergroup Relations." In *Handbook of Industrial and Organizational Psychology Volume 3,* 2nd edition, edited by M. Dunnette and L. Hough, 269–313. Palo Alto, CA: Consulting Psychologists Press.

Hackman, J. 1987. "The Design of Work Teams." In *Handbook of Organizational Behavior,* edited by J. Lorsch, 315–41. Englewood Cliffs, NJ: Prentice-Hall.

Hallam, G., and D. Campbell. 1992. "Selecting Team Members." Paper presented at the annual meeting of the Society of Industrial and Organizational Psychology, Montreal, Quebec, Canada.

Hargrove, R. 1998. *Mastering the Art of Creative Collaboration.* New York: McGraw-Hill.

Haudan, J. 2009. Personal communication with the author, July 11.

Hogan, R. 1992. "Personality and Personality Measurement." In *Handbook of Industrial and Organizational Psychology Volume 2,* 2nd edition, edited by D. Dunnette and L. Hough, 873–919. Palo Alto, CA: Consulting Psychologists Press.

Hogan, R., and R. Blake. 1996. "Vocational Interests." In *Behavior in Organizations,* edited by K. Murphy, 89–114. San Francisco: Jossey-Bass Publishers.

Hogan, R., G. Curphy, and J. Hogan. 1994. "What We Know About Leadership." *American Psychologist* 49 (6): 493–504.

Hogan, R., and J. Hogan. 1994. "The Mask of Integrity." In

Citizen Espionage: Studies in Trust and Betrayal, edited by T. Sarbin, R. Carney, and C. Eoyang. Westport, CT: Praeger.

Hogan, J., and J. Lock. 1995. "A Taxonomy of Interpersonal Skills." Paper presented in Beyond Technical Requirements for Job Performance Symposium, conference of the Society for Industrial and Organizational Psychology, Inc., Orlando, Florida.

Hughes, R. L., R. C. Ginnett, and G. J. Curphy. 2009. *Leadership: Enhancing the Lesson of Experience,* 6th edition. Columbus, OH: McGraw-Hill/Irwin.

Institute of Medicine. 2000. *To Err Is Human: Building a Safer Hospital System.* Washington, DC: National Academies Press.

———. 2001. *Crossing the Quality Chasm: A New Health System for the 21st Century.* Washington, DC: National Academies Press.

———. 2003. *Health Professions Education: A Bridge to Quality.* Washington, DC: National Academies Press.

———. 2009. "Voluntary and Regulatory Measures Needed to Reduce Conflicts of Interest in Medical Research, Education, and Practice." [Online press release; retrieved 9/12/09.] http://policymed.typepad.com/files/iom-press-release-4-28-09.pdf.

Isomura, I. 1998. In *Organizational Behavior,* 4th edition, edited by R. Kreitner and A. Kinicki. New York: Richard D. Irwin.

Kaplan, R. 1991. *Beyond Ambition: How Driven Managers Can Lead Better and Live Better.* San Francisco: Jossey-Bass Publishers.

Katzenbach, J. R., and D. K. Smith. 1993. *The Wisdom of Teams.* Boston: Harvard Business School Press.

Kets de Vries, M., and D. Miller. 1986. "Personality, Culture, and Organization." *Academy of Management Review* 11: 266–79.

Kimball, L., and A. Eunice. 1999. "Virtual Team: Strategies to Optimize Performance." *Health Forum Journal* 42 (4): 59.

Kotter, J. P. 1990. *A Force for Change: How Leadership Differs from Management.* New York: The Free Press.

———. 1996. *Leading Change.* Boston: Harvard Business School Press.

———. 2002. *The Heart of Change.* Boston: Harvard Business School Press.

Kouzes, J., and B. Z. Posner. 1993. *Credibility: How Leaders Gain and Lose It, Why People Demand It.* San Francisco: Jossey-Bass Publishers.

———. 2002. *The Leadership Challenge: How to Get Extraordinary Things Done in Organizations,* 3rd edition. San Francisco: Jossey-Bass Publishers.

Kreitner, R., and A. Kinicki. 1998. *Organizational Behavior,* 4th edition. New York: Richard D. Irwin.

Kushner, H. S. 1986. *When All You've Ever Wanted Isn't Enough.* New York: Summit Books.

Lock, J. 1996. "Developing an Integrative Model of Leadership." Unpublished doctoral dissertation, University of Tulsa, Oklahoma.

———. 1997. "The Relationship Between Trust and Leader–Group Processes." Paper presented in Personality Applications in the Workplace: Thinking Outside the Dots Symposium, 12th annual conference of the Society for Industrial and Organizational Psychology, St. Louis, Missouri.

Lock, J., and L. Thomas. 1998. "The Effects of Leader's Values on Group Citizenship." Poster presented at the 13th annual conference of the Society for Industrial and Organizational Psychology, Dallas, Texas.

Lombardo, M., M. Ruderman, and C. McCauley. 1988. "Explanations of Success and Derailment in Upper-Level Management Positions." *Journal of Business and Psychology* 2: 199–216.

Lorr, M., R. Youniss, and R. Stefic. 1991. "An Inventory of Social Skills." *Journal of Personality Assessment* 57 (3): 506–20.

Mansfield, S. 2009. Personal communication with the author, July 1.

Manz, C., and H. Sims. 1987. "Leading Workers to Lead Themselves." *Administrative Sciences Quarterly* 32: 106–28.

Maurer, R. 1996. *Beyond the Wall of Resistance: Unconventional*

Strategies That Build Support for Change. Austin, TX: Bard Press.

Maxwell, J. C. 1998. *The 21 Irrefutable Laws of Leadership: Follow Them and People Will Follow You*. Nashville, TN: Thomas Nelson Publishers.

McClelland, D. C. 1961. *The Achieving Society*. New York: Free Press.

McKinsey & Company. 1998. "The War for Talent." *Search Connection* 16: 2.

Meglino, B., E. Ravlin, and C. Adkins. 1989. "A Work Values Approach." *Journal of Applied Psychology* 74: 424–32.

Merritt, Hawkins & Associates. 2007. "Report Says Hospitals Employing Physicians in Greater Numbers." [Online article; retrieved 11/23/09.] www.merrithawkins.com/in-the-news.aspx

Merry, M. D. 1996. "Physician Leadership: The Time Is Now!" *Physician Executive* 22 (9).

Northouse, P. G. 2004. *Leadership: Theory and Practice*, 223. Thousand Oaks, CA: Sage Publications.

Peters, T. 1987. *Thriving on Chaos: Handbook for a Management Revolution*. New York: Alfred A. Knopf.

Pfeffer, J. 1998. *The Human Equation: Building Profits by Putting People First*. Boston: Harvard Business School Press.

Pollak, R., and S. Weiner. 1995. "Team Assessment System: Factors of Team Effectiveness." Poster session presented at the conference of the Society for Industrial and Organizational Psychology, Inc., Orlando, Florida.

Price, A. 2009. "Interview with Andrea Price." *Journal of Healthcare Management* 54 (1): 2–4.

Rath, T., and B. Conchie. 2009. *Strengths-Based Leadership*. Omaha, NE: Gallup Press.

Robbins, S. P. 2005. *Essentials of Organizational Behavior,* 8th edition. Upper Saddle River, NJ: Prentice Hall.

Royer, T. 2009. "Foreword." In *The Healthcare C-Suite: Leadership Development at the Top*, by A. N. Garman and C. F. Dye, p. xi. Chicago: Health Administration Press.

Rubinstein, D. 2009. Personal communication with the author, July 9.

Salovey, P., and J. D. Mayer. 1990. "Emotional Intelligence." *Imagination, Cognition, and Personality* 9: 185–211.

Schneider, B. 1987. "The People Make the Place." *Personnel Psychology* 40: 437–53.

Scholtes, P. R. 1998. *The Leader's Handbook: Making Things Happen, Getting Things Done*. New York: McGraw-Hill.

Sherman, V. C. 1993. *Creating the New American Hospital*. San Francisco: Jossey-Bass Publishers.

Showalter, J. S. 2008. *The Law of Healthcare Administration*, 5th edition. Chicago: Health Administration Press.

Singh, K. 2010. "Developing Human Capital by Linking Emotional Intelligence with Personal Competencies in Indian Business Organizations." *International Journal of Business Science and Applied Management* 5 (2). [Online article; retrieved 10/13/09.] www.business-and-manage-ment.org/download.php?file= 2010/5_2—29-42-Singh.pdf.

Smith, D. K. 1996. *Taking Charge of Change: 10 Principles for Managing People and Performance*. New York: Addison-Wesley.

Spears, L. C. 2004. "Practicing Servant Leadership." *Leader to Leader* 34: 7–11.

Stefl, M. 2008. "Common Competencies for All Healthcare Managers: The Healthcare Leadership Alliance Model." *Journal of Healthcare Management* 53 (6): 360–74.

Stogdill, R. 1984. *Stogdill's Handbook of Leadership: A Survey of Theory and Research*. New York: The Free Press.

Tichy, N., and W. Bennis. 2007. *Judgment: How Winning Leaders Make Great Calls*. New York: Portfolio/The Penguin Group.

Weisinger, H. 1998. *Emotional Intelligence at Work: The Untapped Edge for Success*. San Francisco: Jossey-Bass Publishers.

Williams, M. 1975. *The Velveteen Rabbit*. New York: Avon Books.

Williams, S., and F. Jones. 2009. "Transformational Leadership and Servant Leadership: Is There a Difference?" [Online article; retrieved 10/13/09.] http://cnx.org/content/m27080/latest/.

Yukl, G., and D. Van Fleet. 1992. "Theory and Research on Leadership in Organizations." In *Handbook of Industrial and Organizational Psychology Volume 3,* 2nd edition, edited by M. Dunnette and L. Hough, 147–97. Palo Alto, CA: Consulting Psychologists Press.

Zalesnik, A. 1997. "Real Work." *Harvard Business Review* (November–December): 60.

Index

career opportunities, 216–17; servant leaders and, 85

Mid-careerist: complementary work and home life, 214–15; mentoring opportunities, 216–17; networking, 215–16; 360-degree feedback, 215

Mission statement: personal, 206–8; servant leaders and, 83

Multivoting, 200

Negative characteristics, 224, 229, 234

Negative values, 227

Negativity, 124

Network/networking, 97–98, 215–16

Objectives, 44, 94

Optimism, 73

Organization: code of ethics, 55–57; complexity of, 6–7; structure, 29, 30; system, 112; values, 228

Outcomes, 43

Parking lot format, 200

Patient: dissatisfaction, 10; safety, 28

People skills, 65–74

Perception management, 68–69

Performance: focus of review, 86; whole-person evaluation model, 223

Personal attacks, 177

Personal competence, 121

Personal direction, 122

Personal/professional style, 208

Personal relationships, 135

Personality assessment, 130

Physical health, 125

Physician: dissatisfaction, 9; employment, 9; expectations, 8;

perspective, 8–9

Positive characteristics, 224, 229, 234

Positive thinking, 110

Power: balance, 150–51; imbalance, 195; use of, 59

Priorities, 107

Problem solving, 96–97

Process mapping, 200

Process theory, 17–18

Professional development, 84

Protocols, 40, 203–4

Quality of care, 28

Quality improvement, 97

Recognition: of others, 46–47, 69; team, 135

Recruitment, 29

Reference check, 133–34

Reimbursement system, 28

Resistance, 164

Restless discontent, 92

Retirement planning, 217–18

Retreats, 123, 163

Risk, 95

Sacrifices, 109–10

Self-awareness, 47, 119–20

Self-centeredness, 41–42

Self-esteem, 41–42

Self-evaluation: continuing education, 209–10; personal mission statement, 206–8; personal/professional style, 208; values, 209

Self-reflection, 123

Self-tributes, 219

Senior leader: challenges, 27–29; interactions, 33; organizational issues, 29–33

About the Author

**Carson F. Dye, MBA, FACHE,** is an executive search consultant with Witt/Kieffer. He conducts chief executive officer, senior executive, and physician executive searches for a variety of healthcare organizations. His consulting experience includes leadership assessment, organizational design, and physician leadership development. He also conducts board retreats and provides counsel in executive employment contracts and evaluation matters for a variety of client organizations. He is certified to work with the Hogan Assessment Systems tools for selection, development, and executive coaching.

Prior to entering executive search, Mr. Dye was a principal and director of Findley Davies, Inc.'s Health Care Industry Consulting Division. Prior to his consulting career, he served 20 years as chief human resources officer at various organizations, including St. Vincent Medical Center in Toledo, Ohio; The Ohio State University Medical Center in Columbus; Children's Hospital Medical Center in Cincinnati, Ohio; and Clermont Mercy Hospital in Batavia, Ohio.

Mr. Dye is a member of The Governance Institute's Governance One Hundred and also serves as a faculty member for The Governance

Institute. He works as a special advisor to The Healthcare Roundtable and has been named as a physician leadership consultant expert on the LaRoche National Consultant Panel. From 1985 through 2008, he served on the adjunct faculty of the graduate program in management and health services policy at The Ohio State University. Currently, he teaches leadership courses for the Master of Science in Health Administration Program at the University of Alabama at Birmingham.

Since 1989, Mr. Dye has taught several cluster programs for the American College of Healthcare Executives and frequently speaks for state and local hospital associations. He authored the 2001 James A. Hamilton Book of the Year Award winner, *Leadership in Healthcare: Values at the Top* (Health Administration Press, 2000). In addition, he has written *Winning the Talent War: Ensuring Effective Leadership in Healthcare* (Health Administration Press, 2002), *Executive Excellence* (Health Administration Press, 2000), and *Protocols for Health Care Executive Behavior* (Health Administration Press, 1993). With Andy Garman, he co-wrote *Exceptional Leadership: 16 Critical Competencies for Healthcare Executives* (Health Administration Press, 2006). He has written several articles about leadership and human resources that have appeared in various professional journals.

Mr. Dye has had a lifelong interest in leadership and its impact on organizations. He has studied how values drive leadership and affect change management. He is also a student of executive assessment and selection. He earned his BA from Marietta College and his MBA from Xavier University.

About the Contributor

Jared D. Lock, PhD, is a licensed industrial/organizational psychologist. He is president of Carr & Associates, an international consulting firm dedicated to helping organizations maximize human productivity, with a special emphasis on assessing, hiring, on-boarding, and developing executives.

Prior to working at Carr & Associates, Dr. Lock was director of consulting services at Hogan Assessment Systems. He was the lead Hogan consultant on executive-level selection and development, and he regularly partnered with organizational executives and boards concerning selection and development programs. With stints at both Sprint and Jeanneret & Associates, he has more than 15 years of healthcare industry experience. He has been the lead researcher on the development and validation of automated, multi-hurdle, multi-technique selection systems for many *Fortune* 100 organizations. Furthermore, he has created seven unique and proprietary assessments of job-specific performance for various clients throughout the world. In addition, he has been instrumental in implementing leadership development and succession planning programs for several *Fortune* 100 companies, and he has conducted a great deal of research on executive selection and performance.

Dr. Lock has written more than 45 book chapters, papers, and presentations to the professional community. He holds a BA in psychology from the University of Kansas and an MA and a PhD in industrial/organizational psychology from the University of Tulsa.